GARDEN DIY
BOUNDARIES

MURDOCH
B

GARDEN DIY BOUNDARIES

TOBY BUCKLAND

contents

planning a garden landscape

your GARDEN BOUNDARY

The boundary might not be the first thing you think about when designing your garden, but imagine how it feels to sit outside in your garden, enclosed by light-filtering trellis entwined with clematis and fragrant roses and suddenly it takes on a whole new meaning. The right hedge, fence or wall can gift-wrap your garden, making a comfortable and beautiful place to be in and relax.

A combination of ground-cover and hedging entices you to explore.

The importance of boundaries

Boundaries are the key feature of a well-designed garden. They enclose its sides, separate one part from another, and define its focal points and views. Their influence is far-reaching and touches all aspects of gardening, from where the sunshine or shadow falls, to the position of entrances. They even define a garden's atmosphere and how it feels. The right hedge, fence or wall gift-wraps a garden, whereas a poor one distracts from it like peeling paint or ripped packaging.

When I recently moved house, getting a bigger plot of land was definitely the main incentive and stepping out into the new garden was like walking across a giant blank canvas, full of potential but largely empty. A walk out of the back door and across the patio led to the lawn which stretched to a perimeter of hedges and fences – all of which I owned and all of which were overgrown or falling down. Although distant, this motley mix of timber and foliage was the most magnetic part of the garden drawing the eye and making the whole place appear untidy.

One year on and the picture is very different. At the back of the garden, the old hedge remains, but in front a living wall made of willow meanders around. Last March, the willow was cut down from a local osier bed and 20 bundles of red and pea-green whippy sticks arrived. A day of cutting and weaving and piling in topsoil, the ingredients had been turned into a living willow wall, blurring the boundary of the garden with the countryside beyond and demarking the space for a new small orchard.

In a space of just eight yards, the whole feel and function of the garden had been transformed.

That's just one change, there have been many others – a leylandii hedge has been removed in exchange for a close board fence, tumble-down slopes retained with sleepers and bricks plus countless details added to smaller parts of the garden, which have made them more private, luxurious places to sit. One of my favourites is the copper-clad wall – originally just rendered concrete blocks shaped into an arch but with the addition of a piece of copper, cut to size and magically aged, it is now an abstract picture painted in cobalt blue.

But more than simply adding detail, the new boundaries have broken up the garden, engendered the whole place with a sense of mystery and given each individual area a purpose.

Now when you step from the back door, paths between low hedges and walls entice you to explore the orchard, the cut flowers and the tropical garden – each with its own ambience and theme. While, more subtly, gates through internal divides tempt you into secret areas unnoticed until you chance upon them.

Using this book

This book is a practical guide to making your own unique garden boundaries, both around the perimeter of your garden and to divide it into smaller areas. It gives advice on building all kinds of walls, fences and screens, plus information on planting and customizing living boundaries. As well as step-by-step projects and chapters explaining the essential tools, techniques and suppliers, it is packed with original, inspirational photography to help you visualize how new boundaries could work in your own garden.

Consider how you can double up the function of your boundary, as seats or lighting.

The inclusion of an arch and a wrought-iron gate adds a magical touch to this beech hedge.

Boundaries explained

In design terms, boundaries have two major functions. These are physically stopping you in your tracks and/or blocking your view. Most perimeter boundaries form a physical barrier, but that doesn't necessarily mean that they obscure the view of a garden. Indeed, in front gardens the boundary is often low and exists simply to mark a change in property ownership and to discourage trespassers.

Visual boundaries (that block your view) needn't be solid and can be achieved by planting a bushy evergreen in front of a view. You can walk around the evergreen, but from behind its foliage you can't see out and, more importantly, no one can see in.

Design

Applying garden design to boundaries in your garden is largely about deciding the best place for screens and entrances through external divides, and whether views should be blocked or framed. The trick to good garden design isn't just getting things in the right place, though, it's about making them work really hard, so they double up in terms of function and have a lot of style. A retaining wall in the right place and with the right coping, for example, can double up as a seating area. Choosing appropriate materials to fit in with chosen themes and style is just as important.

For most people, many of these decisions are quite instinctive, because of our natural understanding of spaces that feel oppressive and others that feel too exposed. Every garden is different, so decide where you most like sitting in your garden and make your internal boundaries around these spaces. The same instinct comes into play when deciding where entrances should be sited and how high a hedge or fence should be.

This book has been created for inspiration, but primarily as a manual, so use it while you work and don't be afraid to get sawdust and soil between the pages. Good luck!

choosing STYLES

The choice of garden boundaries is huge and although researching through books or on the web will give you an idea of which types are historically accurate or appropriate for your home, the decision is always a tug of war between personal taste and what the budget and the local planning department will allow.

Taste, or knowing what you like, is one thing, but recreating it in your own garden is another and if you're unsure, go on an 'enclosure expedition' checking out the boundaries in other people's gardens. It's no good just looking, you've got to take a mental note of what works and what doesn't and ask yourself why. Do the bricks clash with those used in the house? Are the hedges too imposing? Are the fences poorly built or so lacking in detail that they detract from the garden itself? Once you start, you'll notice the good, the bad and the ugly boundaries in every street, but most importantly, pick up tips and ideas about how to make the ones you like work in your own garden.

A clean-cut serpentine hedge.

The starting point is to think of the purpose you want the boundary to serve and the issues to consider are:

Views

Assess whether there are any features, distant or near, such as church spires or power stations, that you either want to emphasize or obscure. If a boundary is close to you it needn't be very high to hide eyesores in the distance. So, as well as perimeter boundaries, consider using internal screens around seating areas and viewpoints.

Microclimate

Boundaries have a job to do filtering and enhancing the weather, so a stone wall in the right place will hold the heat of the sun well into the evening, while a soil-filled willow wall will always feel cool, benefiting plants that perform best in shady spots. When it comes to buffeting winds, a solid wall is not as effective as one that lets some air through. In fact, a fence with gaps, such as a picket fence or hit-and-miss panel, will slow the wind without creating eddies and turbulence as the air swirls over the top.

Security

Small gardens present the biggest problem when creating a secure boundary because you can't have a high, dominant surround. But even a low, see-through enclosure will discourage cats and dogs from straying onto your property and present a visual deterrent to enter. A tall boundary will not deter a determined thief, but it will stop them eyeing up valuable items in your house and garden and slow their access.

Vertical gardening

Obviously walls and fences provide support for climbers and wall shrubs, but identifying your sunny aspects will give you the opportunity to grow tender or half-hardy, more unusual plants – not just climbers but shrubs and perennials that will thrive in the reflected warmth at its base. In

Pleached hornbeam form a vertical screen.

addition, tall vertical plants can form a boundary in themselves if trained correctly. Some of the projects in this book offer ways to grow plants not just on the boundary but also inside it, due to the soil and built-in irrigation within that keeps plants watered. It's a way of raising up the garden, and ideal if you have a bad back or use a wheelchair as it raises the flowers – bringing them up to sniffing height.

Intimacy

Boundaries can shield seating areas and patios from the gaze of overlooking windows and for the maximum effect, the choice of boundary and its position are key. Where space is limited and sunlight is a premium, as in many city gardens, a close mini-boundary along one side of a patio, rather than the whole area, is often all you need to make a seating area private. For this, the best boundaries are frosted glass screens or flower-covered trellis. Larger gardens can be made private by growing hedges and trees behind fences or around gates or mounding clematis or jasmine, to create an extra 0.6–1m (2–3ft) of foliage screening.

Nestle gates in foliage for an intimate feel.

Noise barriers

The thicker the boundary, the greater its ability to deflect noise. Soil-filled walls, dense hedges or thick wooden sleepers combined with dense planting and foliage, all help to make your space quieter.

Dense foliage creates an effective noise barrier.

Details

Boundaries offer incredible opportunities for detail, from copper cladding to trellis and pretty planting. By using luxurious or unusual materials, even the most tiny areas can be enhanced, leaving ground space free for decorative pots and garden furniture.

Entrances

Enclosures and entrances through them are inseparable, and indeed it's these that make the focal points for vistas and views, and offer opportunities for pretty detailing. An entrance can say a great deal, and, depending on the message you want to get across, be imposing, inviting, prominent or concealed. The primary function of an entrance is of course to provide access, but a gate is a way of giving you that feeling of enclosure in what would normally just be a thoroughfare.

Staggered bamboo screen invites you to enter.

Seating

Boundaries create backdrops and can be a perfect place to position a seat. These may be designed into the boundary, perhaps in the corner of a fence, under a clipped arch in a hedge or on the top of a low retaining concrete block or sleeper wall.

Terracing

Boundaries are a way of retaining soil, transforming sloping gardens into levelled areas that are easier to maintain. They also offer ways of bringing in interest from steps, plinths topped with flowering urns and cascading water features.

Walls can incorporate shallow steps and plants.

choosing MATERIALS

Once you've decided on the function of your boundary, it's time to choose materials and a style that suits your location. Provided different parts of the garden are visually enclosed, so you don't see more than one at a time, you don't need to restrict yourself to just one type of material. Of course, it's best if you can link them in some way by repeating themes.

Treat your house as the most important boundary, dictating the flavour of the area around it, but also absorbing some of the character of the garden. Many designers forget that the house can be used to blend with the garden, as much as the garden should blend with the house. For example, a trellis screen could be made more relevant to the area around the patio by fixing some trellis to the house as well. Or if you are using a copper cladding on a wall (see pages 96–7), repeat the theme in copper-cladded window boxes and sconces.

If you have a new house, often the boundary will be made up of just one type of fencing, but as it is a waste of money to remove it, instead add detail to make it more interesting, for example finials on top of fence posts, paint or trellis cladding.

Internal boundaries can be treated in the same way, provided they have some link, as described.

Materials

There are dozens of materials for garden boundaries, each with their own personality. The criteria for choosing are matching in with your existing materials and themes, preferred style, price and your ability to use them.

Timber

Timber is extremely versatile and is the easiest material to turn into bespoke boundaries because it can be cut to any shape. It's fairly inexpensive too. In a garden, the look is warm and as far as style is concerned, it is a bit of a chameleon – rustic or modern, left rough-hewn or given a lick of paint.

Weathered oak door.

Stone

Natural stone instantly ages a garden and has a feeling of quality. Used with a little imagination, this feeling of antiquity can be enhanced by combining with plants or it can be given a fresh, modern look used with metalwork (see pages 52–3). Local stone is usually the cheapest option and often blends well, but in enclosed areas there is no reason why you can't use other more colourful stone or paint it with a colour of your choice.

Painted render.

Metal

Traditionally, metal is used to give a very formal front face to a garden. Ironwork railings and wrought-iron fences are best left to blacksmiths, but it is possible to use some metals, like sheet copper and wire mesh, in DIY projects with little in the way of tools or specialist knowledge.

The effects that metal creates are fresh and contemporary, and so beautiful they wouldn't be out of place on the walls of an art gallery.

Louvred metal gate.

Living willow fence.

Sandblasted glass screen.

And because metal is relatively cheap to buy, the look comes without a huge price tag.

Stems

Willow and hazel are easy, quick and fun to work and allow you to be really experimental without worry. They also require the least preparation of the materials and while they don't last as long as more robust materials, you can expect 3–6 years out of them. Living willow has the advantage of rooting, and if kept watered, will last indefinitely. If it gets too big, chop it down in the winter.

Glass

Glass is mostly used for detailing in boundaries, for example, stained glass in trellis. If you're looking for a contemporary-style screen, sandblasted safety glass makes an ideal internal boundary that allows light to pass through, and combined with architectural plants, creates interesting silhouettes, in sun or night-time lighting. It equates to the price of a good brick wall, but is quicker to make.

Brick

Brick, with its warm and solid appearance, is the classic boundary material. Its variations are infinite: from the way it is laid to methods of pointing and brick bonds, not to mention the many colours and finishes of the bricks themselves. They do take a certain amount of skill to lay, though with practice, anyone can make a decent low wall. The cost is high, but you can save money when building your own with a few tricks of the trade (see pages 24–5 and 54–5).

Left (top to bottom)
Combination machine-made stock
Combination machine-made stock
New handmade stock
Machine-made Burwell white
London multi-stock reclaimed

Middle (top to bottom)
Reclaimed pot or perforated
Combination multi-stock machine-made
Combination multi handmade reclaimed
Tudor red reclaimed
Handmade soft red

Right (top to bottom)
Staffs blue England
Multi-Tudor red
London yellow stock
Combination handmade reclaimed
Red stock

order OF WORK

Before starting construction, professional builders and landscapers write out the sequence of events needed to get the job done, known as the 'order of works'. It's a time-saver and pre-empts many possible problems, like considering access, storing materials and making sure you've booked hire equipment for the day you need it.

Planning ahead

• Stacking materials – if you intend to build a boundary over a period of a number of months, it won't be appropriate to leave the materials on the lawn. It is much better to organize deliveries for when you need them.

• Hire equipment – whether it's a drill, a cement mixer or a skip, it's important to get them when you have the time to do the work, so order in advance.

• Delivery dates and times – make sure it won't be inconvenient to take time off work, or if you aren't there, that you've given exact instructions about where the delivery is to be placed to avoid coming home to find that your parking space is taken by 4 tonnes (80cwt) of sand!

• Noise – always check with neighbours when it's okay to have deliveries and use loud machinery and power tools.

• Access – what is the quickest way and least troublesome route from where materials are delivered and where you want to use them? Are there any short-cuts? For example, by temporarily removing a fence panel, you can speed up the process.

• Timing – if you're building more than just boundaries, maybe putting in a path or patio too, examine which has the deepest footings. (Because a wall has deeper footings than a path, it is always built before you put down paving.) Trellis, on the other hand, doesn't, so it's best to put it in afterwards to keep access open and avoid damaging what you've just done.

Estimating materials

Once you've decided on your boundary – its style, materials and design – you need to estimate quantities and buy the materials. This is something that all good builders' merchants will be able to help with, provided you know what materials you want. So, arm yourself with knowledge – shop around, have a look at materials, take a photo of your garden or features to help you match materials or pictures from books or magazines that you are trying to copy. Visit salvage yards and metalwork shops, places you might not ordinarily go to, for inspiration.

Estimate how much of each material you will need.

Inevitably, you will have to modify designs from pictures and step-by-steps to fit your location, particularly if you are making some of the bespoke projects, such as trellis (see pages 88–91). Draw a sketch of your idea or, better still, a scale drawing, so you can accurately quantify yourself. Scale drawings are done with a scale ruler that shows every 1m (3ft) represented as 1–10cm (⅓–4in), depending on how detailed you want the drawing. Remember that if you are building anything from timber, and it involves a lot of cutting to length, add an extra 10 per cent for waste.

The following are typical quantities for standard boundaries:

Walls

• 1 tonne (20cwt) of sand/ballast equals 0.75 cubic m in volume.
• For concrete foundations you need six and a half 25kg (½cwt) bags of cement per tonne (20cwt) of ballast.
• For 1m (3ft) of single skin wall you need 60 bricks, or 120 for a full brick wall plus 10 for breakages.

• For 1m (3ft) of concrete block wall (using standard 100mm [4in] blocks laid on their sides) you need 21 blocks.
• 1 tonne (20cwt) of sand combined with eight bags of cement is enough to lay approximately 12.5m (41½ft) of full brick walling or 30m (96ft) of concrete blocks.

Close board fence

For every linear metre (3ft) of close board fence you need eight 150mm (6in) feather boards.

Feather boards.

Willow

One standard bundle of willow makes approximately 0.5m (1½ft) square of willow wall.

Willow wall.

Stone

You get 4 square metres (40 square feet) of wall per tonne (20cwt) of Dressed York stone.

Dressed York stone.

How to buy

If previously you have concentrated on small-scale garden jobs, you'll be accustomed to buying materials in small bags and taking them home in the car. For larger jobs, you'll have a choice of how to get it delivered to your home, depending on the material in question. This has an implication on cost.

Buying stone, gravel and ballast

Stone, gravel, sand and ballast are all cheapest to buy delivered loose, but that leaves you with the problem of storage and cleaning up and, for instance, builders' sand will stain a driveway, so must be contained on plastic sheeting. Slightly more expensive but far more convenient are large, white aggregate bags or pallets. This is definitely the best option if the job is going to take a while because it keeps out cats and weather, and looks neater.

Buying bricks.

Buying timber

Timber is sold in standard lengths and sizes, depending on the type of wood. This could be 3m (10ft) and 5m (16ft) for example, so if your job involves cutting it down to 2.5m (8ft) lengths, ascertain the standard sizes before buying to ensure you are not paying for waste. Timber is readily available from timber/builders' merchants or, for older, more interesting wood, check out salvage yards.

Timber is delivered in individual planks, so if there is a lag time before installing it, keep it flat to prevent it from bowing. It is also important to protect it from the wet or it may twist out of shape.

Buying timber from a salvage yard.

tools and techniques

marking OUT

Marking out is the process of transferring the pencilled features on a garden design into lines on the ground and creating reference points allowing speedy and accurate construction. It also allows you one last chance to alter your plans. Marking out is a job that is worth taking time over and getting right, as any errors can make building and quantifying problematic.

Making a 3:4:5 triangle

Creating a right angle on paper is easily done with a set square, but to transfer this onto the ground you need to do a little maths. It's not complicated, though, and getting it right now will make things much easier for you later.

The technique was discovered by the Greek mathematician Pythagoras some 2500 years ago and involves making a triangle on the ground. If the base is 3m (9ft) long (the units don't matter as long as they are all the same), the side 4m (12ft) and the diagonal 5m (15ft), the corner where the base and side connect will be a perfect right angle. The quickest way to mark this is with 12m (36ft) of measuring tape looped around a triangle of bamboo canes pushed into the ground. Hold the ends of the zero and 12m (36ft) mark of the tape next to one cane and move the other canes to the 4m (12ft) and 9m (27ft) mark to get your right angle.

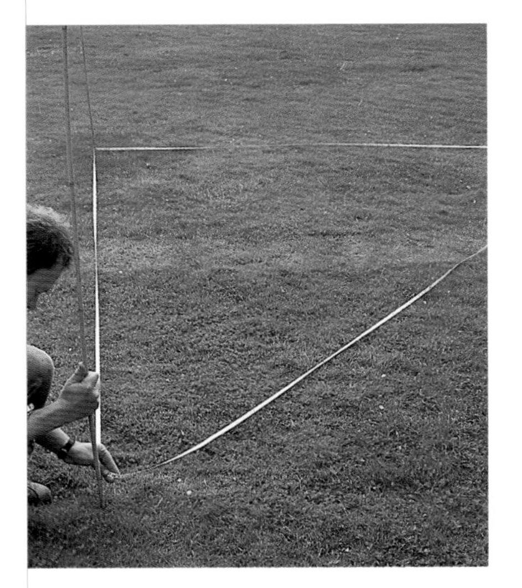

Make a 3:4:5 triangle.

External boundaries and not offending the neighbours

Boundary disputes are one of the main causes of conflict between neighbours, therefore it is essential to check deeds of ownership before commencing work on any perimeter boundary. It is also prudent to liaise with neighbours first about any changes you are making and to get permission to enter their garden while working on the divide. If you are replacing a fence, always build to the line of the old one and get your neighbours to confirm that your string marking lines are in the right place.

Marking and fixing fence posts

To mark out the line of a fence, fix the two end fence posts in position and run a taut line between their bottoms – you may need to tie back any overhanging branches or herbaceous plants that get in its way.

Starting at one end, mark the position of the intermediate fence posts. (Depending on the design of the fence, the fence posts will either occur down its centre or be on the owner's side, so that the flat face of the fence runs along the boundary.) If any coincide with a drain or old concrete footing, digging a hole or hammering in a fence spike will be impossible, so either move all of the post positions along to avoid the obstacle or, if you are building a picket or close board fence, have a longer arris rail for that one section.

Mark positions of posts on the ground.

If you are building a panel fence, moving the position of the fence posts will more than likely mean that the end panels have to be cut down to fit the run (see pages 26 and 27).

If you're concreting the posts, dig the holes for all of the intermediate posts, making them 600mm (24in) deep and 150–200mm (6–8in) wide. Then, run another string line between the two end posts at their tops. If the end posts are upright, then when each intermediate fence post is brought up against the top and bottom string line, it will be upright too. Finally, check that it is level side to side before bracing and concreting in place.

Use a taut line to position the posts.

Scribing an arc using a cane and string

Curved patios and paths, and the boundaries that flank them, produce an informal look that blends well with planting. Walls that double up as seating benefit from being curved as they allow people to face each other when seated, and because they are curved, their stability is increased.

You can mark a serpentine or curved line on the ground by eye, but it is difficult to make it look natural. A more reliable method is to tie a length of string to a cane pushed in at the centre of your arc. Hold the string taut at the point you want the radius and use it as a guide as you spray ground marking paint or sprinkle sand along your line.

Scribe an arc.

Rather than being arbitrary about the position of the curves, aim to arc them around existing features of a garden, for example trees and seating areas, as this helps to unify and tie the features in a garden together.

Using fence spikes

Fence spikes take away all the hard work of digging holes. After marking out the position of the posts, use a sledgehammer to drive the fence spikes into the ground. Custom-made, plastic driving units are available which fit into their tops and take the impact of the hammer, preventing damage to the spike. These also have metal bars, which allow you to knock them back into line if they start to twist.

The trick to getting fence spikes upright is to check with a spirit level after every few blows with the hammer.

If they need straightening, hammer the driver against the direction they lean to bring them upright. Once in the ground, hammer the post into the socket of the fence spike while ensuring that it is firm and upright. The best fence post systems have bolts which let you tighten the metal around the base of the post. These allow a little movement, making it easy to get the posts perfectly upright.

Use a level to check the fence spikes are upright.

Tighten the fence posts in position.

As well as spikes, there are many different metal fence fixings including sockets for bolting the base of a post to concrete, spikes that drive into the hole left after a rotten fence post has snapped and sockets for extending the height of your fence. They all work well, but if you use them, aim to disguise all metal spikes and fixings beneath evergreen planting or below soil.

concrete, MORTAR AND FOUNDATIONS

This section is about the two glues that hold the hard landscaping in a garden together – concrete and mortar. Understanding how to make and use them is an essential part of many garden DIY projects, including building walls, setting fence posts, laying paving and making water features.

The ingredients

Concrete and mortar have different applications. Mortar is used to fix materials such as bricks and paving stones to a level, while concrete is used for the foundations of walls, paths and fence posts.

Sharp sand

A washed sand with angular grains that fills the spaces between stones in concrete. Because their sides are angular, they lock together giving concrete its strength. A mortar made from sharp sand and cement makes a wear-resistant mix for laying and pointing paving stones, but is too stiff and hard to work for bricklaying.

Cement

The bonding agent that holds both concrete and mortar together. It is a caustic grey powder containing limestone, which crystallizes and hardens when mixed with water.

Ballast

A combination of sharp sand and gravel used in concrete mixes. A mix of 3:1 (three parts crushed stone or gravel, and one part sharp sand) works well. It is also known as all-in aggregate.

Building sand

Sand with rounded grains used to make mortar. Because they are round, they roll over each other, making it easier to tap bricks and concrete blocks down to level. It also contains a small amount of clay which makes it more pliable and sticky when wet.

Mortar and concrete mixes

Making concrete or mortar is like baking – you need a recipe and the ingredients in the right amounts. These are expressed as a ratio, for example 1:6 – the cement the smallest number.

When mixing, always measure quantities using a levelled-off bucket, not a shovel. Because you are constantly making new mixes, consistency throughout the job ensures that concrete is strong and that the joints in brickwork dry to the same colour. To make concrete for a foundation you need to make a 1:5 mix of cement and ballast. You can mix this by hand in a wheelbarrow or on a sheet of plywood, but it's easier and quicker with a cement mixer. To mix by hand, measure out five level buckets of ballast and place on a sheet of plywood. Sprinkle a bucket of cement over the top and turn with a shovel until the mix is an even grey colour. Create a crater in the mix and part fill with water, turning in the edges until the mix is wet and soft but not sloppy.

With a mechanical mixer, water is added first followed by the cement to form a slurry. This ensures that the ballast is completely coated as it is shovelled into the mixer. Add water with the ballast as necessary and mix for at least two minutes to obtain a uniform consistency.

Masonry mortar consists of 1:5 parts cement and building sand for above ground work and 1:3 for courses below soil level. It can be mixed by hand as above, but for large jobs hire a mechanical mixer to save

Mix mortar until the consistency is sticky.

time and your back. Add water until it becomes smooth but stiff enough to hold its shape when furrowed up with a trowel. Once the right consistency has been achieved, mix for a few minutes to create small air bubbles in the mortar. These help to make it workable and sticky. A test to see whether it is the correct consistency for bricklaying is to scoop a little onto a trowel, shake off any excess and turn upside down. If the mortar falls off, it either needs more water or mixing.

Black mortar highlights the red bricks.

Additives are available including dyes which create coloured joints in brickwork and plasticizers which increase the air bubble content of mortar, making it more forgiving to lay and easier to mix to the correct consistency. Plasticizers can be bought premixed into the cement or as liquid for adding as you mix.

Plasticizer increases the air bubble content of mortar.

Foundations

For walls under 1m (3ft) high, the depth of the concrete footing should be at least 215mm (8½in) and never less than the thickness of the wall. The width of the foundation depends on how wide the wall is and whether it is a retaining wall. Freestanding walls require a footing between two and three times their width while retaining walls demand a footing at least three times their width.

1 When digging the foundations use lines to mark out the width of the footing and dig down until you reach solid subsoil. The sides of the hole should be vertical, the ends square and the base at least 100mm (4in) deeper than the required depth of concrete (this allows the foundations to be buried out of sight).

2 Before pouring the concrete, hammer wooden pegs along the centre of the trench to the depth you want the concrete and check that they are all the same height using a spirit level. The pegs become a guide ensuring that the concrete is poured and smoothed to the correct level making it strong and flat, which makes it much easier to lay bricks/blocks once it has dried.

3 Pour the concrete to the tops of the pegs, slicing with a shovel to release any trapped air and screed to the tops of the pegs with a length of timber. Because the concrete shrinks as it hardens, leave for at least two days before starting construction.

slopes and DRAINAGE

Changes of level, enclosed by hedges or judiciously planted evergreens, can blur the boundaries of a garden making it seem bigger while at the same time hiding all but its best views and features. Boundaries across a slope can create a sense of mystery too. Where levels are changed, consideration has to be given to drainage.

Measuring slopes

One of the biggest worries for DIYers is knowing the quantity of materials to order, known as quantifying, but if you have measured up accurately, you will get all the help you need from builders' merchants. Measuring the length, height and width of the boundary is easy but it gets complicated if the ground is sloping and you want to build a wall into it. To calculate the 'falls', i.e. how much the ground slopes, there are two methods.

Over a short distance place a 2m (6½ft) straight-edged plank at the top of the slope, hold it out with a level on the top so it reaches over the bottom of the slope. When it is level with the base, then measure from the base to the plank to give you the fall.

Use a plank and a spirit level to measure a fall.

For longer, gentle slopes, hammer in a post at the top of the slope and fix the top of the hose at 1m (3ft) high onto the post. Take the other end of the hose to the bottom of the slope and fill with water from a can. When it is full to the brim at both ends, they are level.

The fall is the measurement taken from the top of the hose to the ground at the bottom of the slope, less 1m (3ft).

Use a hose to measure a fall over long distances.

Fences and slopes

Picket, post and rail and close board fences can all be built to follow the contours of a slope perfectly. Panel fencing, because it comes in large 180cm (6ft) sections will not and instead forms steps between each panel. Such steps are useful for making particularly large jumps in level but are best avoided as they look sharp and don't blend with the land they enclose. If you have a slope, the choice is between a close board and a picket fence that undulates with the ground or, if the slope is gentle, the fence can have a level top and an undulating base. Whichever you choose, for strength, always make the fence posts and the pickets/feather boards upright, sloping only the arris rails.

Walls and slopes

The large old walls surrounding stately homes were often built to follow the rises and falls in the land. Despite their longevity, such walls do not meet modern building standards as they have shallow foundations and are stuck together with soft lime mortar. This seemingly weak construction actually accounts for their strength allowing the wall to move as the soil shifts beneath their footings. The building of sloping walls is best left to specialists.

Retaining walls

While a gently rising lawn may be easy to live with, a patio needs to be level and this means terracing into the slope and building retaining walls to hold back the soil.

Lining

If retaining walls aren't lined on the inside, the appearance of the bricks can be spoilt with a covering of white powder. This happens because water from the soil seeps into the bricks, carrying salts with it. When it reaches the face of the wall, the water evaporates and the salt is left behind. Water seeping through a wall will also make it vulnerable to algae which looks particularly bad on render and will make it prone to frost damage.

There are three ways to seal the back of a retaining wall from moisture. It can be given a coat of bitumastic paint, which is a modern quick drying version of pitch. On the down side, it is expensive and to get an even coat, the wall needs to be smooth.

Water-proof bitumastic paint.

Another effective method of lining is to cover the back of the wall with a waterproof cement sand/render available from any builders' merchant. It is time consuming but a good way of sealing where brickwork is sloppy, as lumpy mortar between the joints provides a good key.

The most economical way to seal the back of a wall is with plastic damp proof membrane (DPM). This tucks down against the wall and is held in place by the infill. Its only disadvantage is that it does not make a good seal around weep holes (see below).

Drainage

As well as holding back soil, a retaining wall slows down the movement of water and unless adequate provision for drainage is included, the ground above it will be wetter than it was before the wall was built.

Good drainage can be achieved in two ways. Firstly, weep holes are lengths of 15mm (¾in) plastic pipes cut to the width of the wall and laid every 900mm (3ft) between bricks in the second course above ground level.

Lay weep holes between bricks in the second course.

Better looking but more complicated is a land drain. This is a perforated 100mm (4in) wide pipe, set in gravel or sulphate-free hardcore, on a slope of 1:70. The pipe connects to a land drain, known as a soakaway, which consists of buried rubble that acts as a sump from which water is absorbed into the soil.

Lay the drainage pipe and connect with land drain.

Soakaways should be located near the end of the wall but always at least 5m (16ft) away from buildings and a good distance from utilities such as drains, sewers and gas pipes. Whichever method you use, before backfilling the wall, line the soil behind it with a 'geotextile layer'. This is a fibrous material that keeps the soil particles from blocking the drainage pipes.

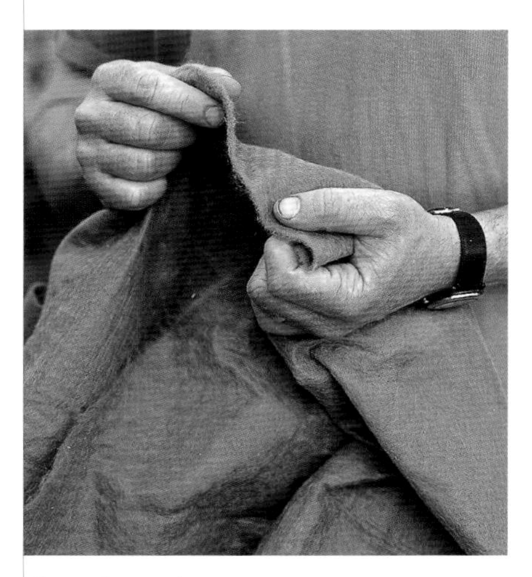

Geotextile membrane.

Backfill the bottom half of the wall with a washed gravel or sulphate-free hardcore and fold the geotextile layer over its top, before filling to the top of the wall with soil.

bricks and BRICKLAYING

Bricklaying, like most crafts, involves many different skills that are simple on their own but when put together can seem daunting. However, by following the advice in this section and the projects on pages 42 to 57 you will be armed with all the knowledge you need to build freestanding and retaining garden walls up to 700mm (27½in) height.

Brick types

Common bricks – economical bricks with uneven colour and texture manufactured for use where they won't be seen (for example, foundation work, internal construction and inside retaining walls.)

Engineering bricks – strong clay bricks with low water absorption for damp-proof courses and coping.

Facing bricks – bricks manufactured for display with few blemishes, even colour and surface texture.

Cutting bricks

Mark around the brick where you want to cut it and sit it on a layer of sand, edge side up. Using a bolster and a club hammer, strike the brick first on one edge then the other, going back and forth between the two until it fractures in half.

Cutting bricks using a bolster and club hammer.

Marking out

When building a brick wall, always chalk a line on the foundations to mark the face side and ends. To save having to cut bricks, make the length of the wall a multiple of the length of a brick 215mm (8½in) plus width of the joint 10mm (½in). Work this out on paper or lay a dry course of stretcher bricks (see below) on the foundations leaving 10mm (½in) spaces between them to get your dimensions.

Laying the first course

Next set the end stretcher bricks in position on a trowel of mortar, tapping them down until the mortar beneath is 10mm (½in) thick and the tops are level with each other. Ascertain this by bridging between them with a taut line or a straight-edged length of timber and sitting a spirit level on top.

With the end bricks in place, run a line between them to mark their top front edge, holding it in position beneath two more bricks. This speeds up the rate of laying considerably, allowing the bricks in the centre of the wall to be tapped level lengthways by eye. You then only have to use a spirit level to check across the wall.

Trowel mortar on the inside of the line and ripple its surface by zig-zagging the trowel's point along its length, creating a central channel. This spreads the mortar to the width of a brick and makes tapping the bricks level much easier.

Trowelling mortar.

Buttering the end of a brick.

Turn the mortar to get plenty of air into it and trowel a small amount on to the end of the brick smoothing the mortar to its edges. If the mortar keeps falling off, the mortar is too dry. Rectify this by splashing a small amount of water onto the mortar and turn it in with a trowel.

Laying subsequent courses

Position the buttered brick up to the line and push it against the end brick to create a 10mm (½in) joint between them. Tap each brick down with the handle of a club hammer or trowel, until it is level front to back and its top edge is level with the line. Repeat this process until all of the face skin of bricks are in place (the last brick will need to be buttered on both ends). Lay the bricks at the back of the wall leaving a 10mm (½in) gap between the two skins (see below) checking for level across the wall as you go. Fill the gap with mortar and start the next course with two header bricks one at each end of the wall. Again, check that the joint is 10mm (½in), a storey rod is useful for this (see page 33), and run a line between them to mark their top edge. Now cut a 'queen closure' brick

Laying a queen closure brick.

and lay this next, to break the vertical joint and continue laying until the next course is complete.

Build up the ends of the wall first to support the builders' line and lay the bricks in the centre course by course.

Laying the second course.

As you work, collect the mortar that oozes out as the bricks are tapped down by running the point of the trowel along the face of the brick below, pulling excess mortar onto the trowel's blade. This and any that falls onto the foundations can be put back onto the mortar board for later use.

Leave any mortar that gets onto the face of the bricks until it stiffens (this takes an hour or so depending on the weather), then scrape it off with a trowel.

Pointing the joints

Next 'point' the joints, which involves smoothing over the dips and pits in the mortar to keep water out and make them frost-proof.

For walls in exposed positions you can make what is called a 'weather struck joint' by pressing a pointing trowel held at an angle down the vertical joints then across the vertical joints.

Weather-struck pointing.

Bricklaying jargon explained

Stretchers – bricks laid lengthways along the wall.

Headers – bricks laid sideways through the wall to bond the sides together.

Half bat – a brick cut in half across the middle.

Queen closure – a brick cut in half lengthways.

Joint – the mortar between the bricks.

Course – a row of bricks/blocks/stones in a wall.

Frog – an indentation moulded into the tops of some bricks, gripping them into the wall and making laying easier.

Single/half brick wall – a wall 102.5mm (4⅛in) wide (the width of a brick).

Full/double brick wall – a wall 215mm (8½in) wide (the length of a brick).

Soldier course – bricks laid on edge usually as a coping.

Coping – a protective top to a wall that stops rainwater from soaking into the bricks and making them soft and prone to frost damage.

Skin – the front or back course of stretcher bricks in a full brick wall.

'Buttering' – a term used to describe placing mortar on the ends of a brick for the vertical joints in a wall.

using TIMBER

Timber is versatile, relatively inexpensive and you don't need the carpentry skills of a furniture maker to create beautiful wooden boundaries. With a few basic tools, a little know-how and a tin of coloured wood stain, you can build a fence that captures the character of your garden while giving you and your plants shelter.

Timber joints

For many of the projects in this book it is necessary to make simple timber joints to fasten lengths of wood together in a neat, strong way. While making joints takes a little time, it is easy to do and the finished result is far more attractive than when more expensive metal brackets are used.

Half-lapped/notch joints

These joints allow two pieces of timber to cross and yet still be flush with one another. They are useful when building gate frames and for notching the arris rails of close board fences into their supporting posts.

To make a half lap joint

1 Lay the timbers across one another and mark both pieces where you want the joint. Then mark the depth of the joint. This needs to be half the depth of the timber if they are the same size or half the depth of the thinnest length.

2 To make chiselling out the wood easier, make repeated cuts through each timber to the depth of the joint with approximately 10mm (½in) between them. (The fastest way to do this is with a circular saw set to the depth of the joint, but it is easy to do with a wood saw.)

3 Remove the remaining wood from the joint with a broad chisel.

Mortice joints

Basically, these joints involve one piece of timber slotting into another, like a key in a lock. They are useful when making post and rail fences, close board fences where you want the posts to be visible from both sides and attaching picket fences to gate posts. To speed up the process, sharpen the ends of the arris rails into points to reduce the amount of wood you need to chisel from the post.

1 Mark on the fence post where you want the joint to be positioned. (Reduce its size if the arris rails are sharpened as above.)

2 Drill a series of holes through the post where you want the joint.

3 Chisel out the waste, slot in the arris rails, pinning them in place with a nail or screw.

Fixing timber with screws and nails

To prevent wood splitting, always drill pilot holes before tightening in screws. To avoid the bother of constantly changing the bits, borrow or hire an extra electric screwdriver so that you have one for the pilot bit and one for the screwdriver. Always use galvanized or coated nails and screws, as untreated types rust, leaving stains on the face of the timber.

Painting and preserving

Most shop-bought fence panels are supplied ready-treated with preservative for a 15–25 year lifespan. But if you buy timber to build your own bespoke fence, you can use untreated wood, as long as you're prepared to coat it yourself with a wood stain or paint. This said, it always pays to buy pressure-treated timber for any part of the fence that will be in contact with the ground such as posts and gravel boards.

You can dramatically cut down the time it takes to paint a large fence by hiring a paint sprayer. It's ideal for painting the fiddly struts of trellis too.

Fences and trees

If there is a tree growing along the line where you want to build a fence, don't nail the fence directly to it as when the tree sways in the wind, so will the fence, plus the health of the tree will be damaged. Instead, put a post a metre or so back from the trunk and cantilever two arris rails to within several centimetres of it. For effect, a false post can go on the end propped in place by a diagonal timber spiked into the ground behind the tree. Where there are branches, dips or holes can be cut in the fence allowing

Situate posts well back from trees.

room for them to move in the wind – instead of an inconvenience, the tree will give your fence character.

Cutting down a fence panel

At the end of a fence run it is often necessary to cut down a panel in order to turn a corner or connect the fence in with a building.

1 Draw a line down the fence where you want the cut.

2 Screw a length of 50 x 20mm (2 x ¾in) batten to each side of the fence along the line.

Sawing the fence panel to size.

3 Cut the fence down with a saw.

Curved fences

To create a curve, use timber thin enough to be bent into an arc for the arris rails. To give the arris strength and to hold its shape it needs to be laminated. Bend it around a series of posts temporarily hammered into the ground around the arc, fixing it to the two end posts with a screw. Then paint the outer face with external wood glue and bend another length of wood over the top, screwing it in place as you go. Allow the glue to set before detaching and fixing in position.

Fencing jargon explained

Gravel boards – commonly used to underpin panel and close board fences. They form a barrier between the ground and the main fence, taking all the weather and rotting first.

Arris rails – sometimes called stringers, these are timbers that run between the posts and have pickets or feather-edged boards hammered to them.

Feather-edged boards – timber planks that are wedge-shaped in cross section to allow them to overlap each other.

incorporating PLANTS

Plants bring seasonality, character and individuality to even the most mundane of spaces and therefore deserve as much thought and care as any boundary detail. This section has been included to help you choose the right plants for your boundaries and to get them off to the best possible start.

Hedges

Planting a hedge is the quickest and most economical way to enclose a large area. Before planting, dig or rotavate along the line of your intended hedge, incorporating a barrow load of garden compost, well-rotted horse manure or garden centre bought soil improver every 4–5m (13–16ft). Then, plant your hedge, firming in the roots and water in.

The trick to getting hedges to establish quickly is to water through the growing season, particularly during dry spells in their first year after planting. To encourage the hedge to fill out, lightly trim the sides in early summer of the second year. Although it's tempting to plant the hedge and leave it to grow and reach the height you want before cutting it back, it's better to trim its top half a metre or so below the desired height, to encourage it to branch out and fill out more quickly. And, once the hedge is at the desired height it will be easier to trim as it prevents the formation of difficult-to-cut thick branches.

A smart, low front garden hedge.

With most hedges, you can get away with one major prune at the end of summer. This gives them time to put on a fresh flush of leaves for winter, while removing unwanted growth. But for the neatest look, especially with hedges such as box (*Buxus*), yew (*Taxus*) and topiary features, it's best to give a quick prune after the last frost in late spring and then again in late summer. When trimming hedges over 1–1.2m (3–4ft), always make the sides slope inwards slightly to give the hedge an A-shaped profile. Otherwise, the top of the hedge will cast shadow over the base, making it gappy.

Climbers and wall shrubs

To soften brand new fences and walls, climbers and wall shrubs are the obvious choice. The range is vast, so first decide what you want your climber to do – flowers, berries, scent, evergreen or deciduous, autumn colour? Most of us want all of these things but that's impossible from just one plant. However, by combining a couple you can have it all. Next, ascertain what will grow in front of the boundary. Even if you are unsure of your gardening knowledge, garden centres and nurseries can help you choose, if you find out the following:

Climbers soften the square edges of a panel fence.

- Aspect – which way it faces (whether it catches the morning or afternoon sun or none at all).
- Soil – sandy and free-draining, or clay-rich and sticky? Take a sample to the garden centre for advice.
- Exposure – is it very hot and prone to dry out or very windy?
- What do the neighbours grow well, because often similar plants will do well for you.

• Size and space – how much area do you need to fill, including base and top?
• How wet or dry is the soil? Does it sit puddled in winter and crack in the heat of summer, or is it permanently boggy or dry?

Bear in mind that climbers grow in different ways. Clematis will establish on top of the support, forming a cloud of foliage and flowers, so plant herbaceous perennials or smaller shrubs, like lavender (*Lavandula*), to fill the gap. Honeysuckles (*Lonicera*) and jasmine (*Jasminum*) become great sprawling mounds in front of the support and often look their best when they cascade over from the other side, so a good choice for internal divides. Wisteria, climbing roses (*Rosa*) and vines (*Vitis*) all lend themselves to training, allowing you to clothe the boundary as you want.

If you are building around a well-established plant, then you can always plan for it in your boundary design.

A scalloped wall to highlight the position of a tree.

Planting at the base of a boundary

Life at the base of a wall or fence is harsh, potentially in a rain shadow and what moisture there is can be sapped up by the boundary. So, give plants a good start by digging in lots of garden compost or garden centre bought soil improver to increase the soil's water-holding capacity. This will help drainage in wetter soils too. Plants bought in containers (as opposed to bare-root) won't grow into the surrounding soil for a few weeks, so need a reservoir of easily accessible water. Before planting, soak the root ball in a bucket of water until the air has bubbled out.

Then, dig your hole, at least 500mm (20in) from the base of the boundary to enable it to root into better soil away from footings and to give the roots space to grow. Sometimes it's hard to give plants enough water, so cut a plastic bottle in half, take off its lid and sink it into the soil, to act like a funnel, directing water to the roots.

This plastic bottle directs water down to the roots.

Using supports or self-clinging plants

Some climbers like Virginia creepers (*Parthenocissus*), climbing hydrangea and ivies (*Hedera*) are self-clinging and need only to be directed towards the boundary to pull themselves up. Others like roses, passion flowers (*Passiflora*) and honeysuckles require a support to wind around. Wires, fixed at 450mm (18in) intervals horizontally up the support, are a far better choice than trellis. Unless it's used carefully, trellis can spoil the look of a boundary and is unsuitable for many climbers. Wires, on the other hand, are discreet and versatile, running in any direction. They are also easier to remove if you need to maintain the boundary behind. Some climbers, such as clematis and honeysuckle, will weave in front and behind the wire, but where you are training climbers, try to avoid tucking stems behind the wire as it makes them difficult to move later.

Fixing vine eyes

Wires need to be held on a support with 100–150mm (4–6in) hooks, which are screwed into the boundary, and are called 'vine eyes'. These hold the climber about 50mm (2in) away from the support, and allow air to circulate behind, helping to prevent fungal diseases, such as mildew. Always choose plastic-coated wire and tighten them in place using 'bolt tensioners' at the end of each horizontal wire. Or you can use vine eyes on their own to pin individual stems in place, tying the branches to each vine eye with soft twine.

good WORKING PRACTICE

When time is spent moving materials that are in the way or looking for tools, construction jobs become fraught, and the fun goes out of building them. This is why organizing your tools and materials before starting any of the projects in this book is essential, enabling you to carry them out swiftly, safely and to a high standard. And of course enjoy building them too!

Personal safety

Your own safety, and that of others is the primary consideration when building any garden project. To protect yourself, wear strong gloves when handling materials with sharp or splintered edges such as stone, brick and timber, and always wear them when handling cement. Safety goggles are essential when cutting stone and bricks and should be combined with a mask when spray painting. One of the most common injuries occurs when tools or heavy materials fall on your feet, so always wear steel toe-cap boots. To protect your back, lift properly facing the object as you pick it up with your knees bent and your back straight. Finally, don't overdo it. If you're not used to physical work, take your time and, if possible, persuade friends to help you. As with most gardening jobs, working with someone else always more than doubles the speed at which the job is done, especially when doing hard manual work, such as digging foundations or carrying materials.

Always lift with your knees bent.

Site safety

Because boundaries tend to be relatively large, you're going to have to bring a lot of materials into your garden. Make sure that access is easy by tying back shrubs and trees that would get in your way as materials are barrowed through and use planks of wood supported on bricks to ramp up low steps. Taking time to make the access to your garden as open as possible will make carrying the materials easier and safer.

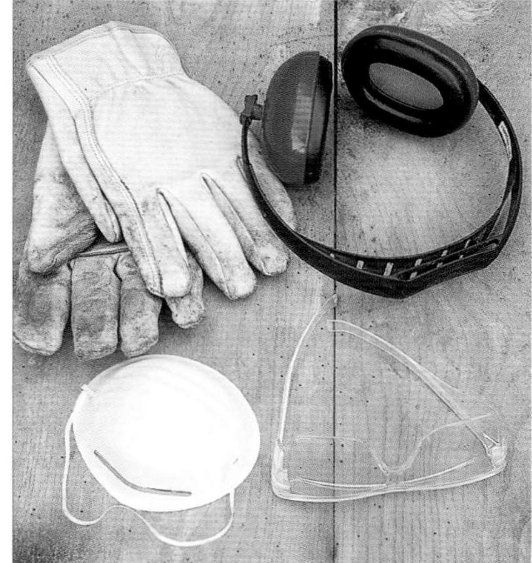

Safety equipment.

Use planks as ramps on steps.

Treat moving materials as a separate job to the construction, stacking them in neat, stable piles near to where you need them. Doing this prevents unnecessary legwork during construction and means materials won't topple over.

If you or your neighbours have children and you are replacing a perimeter boundary, they must be considered at all times. To a child, a stack of bricks, power tools, chisels and hammers present an irresistible opportunity for fun. So, ensure that tools are kept well out of their reach and if necessary cordon off your working area with a temporary plastic fence.

> **Safety at-a-glance**
>
> Always lift properly with your knees bent and your back straight.
>
> Be sure to wear steel toecap boots.
>
> When cutting stone and bricks always wear goggles.
>
> Strong gloves must be worn when handling materials with sharp or splintered edges.
>
> Keep all tools well out of reach of children and cordon off your working area with a temporary plastic fence.

Tools

The list of tools you need is included with each of the projects. If you don't own them, hire them – the extra cost is worth paying as it will make building much easier. If you hire tools, book a few days before you need them along with any attachments, such as saw blades and safety equipment necessary. When they are delivered, read the instructions and spend a little time practising how to use them.

Check that all the tools you need are in working order and at the end of each day clean and store them away in a secure place where you can easily lay your hands on them the next day.

Cleaning off a trowel at the end of the day.

Organizing your work

Give yourself plenty of room, so that you can work comfortably. Do this by allocating different parts of your garden to different jobs involved in the construction of your boundary. For example, create a space for a workbench that allows you to move freely around it especially if you are cutting timber. Allocate another for mixing mortar. This should be near where the sand is delivered, in an open spot that is easy to barrow to and from, and where splashes of cement from the mixer won't cause any damage. For projects such as building trellis, screens and gates, you also need a space to lay them flat while you work. This can be a drive, patio or lawn, but should be as near as possible to their finished location.

As you work, stand back from the job regularly to check that string lines are level and in the correct place and to help you plan the next stage. The trick to building things well is to be methodical and give yourself plenty of time to enjoy what is a creative process and to make sure each stage is finished properly before moving on to the next.

The other thing to remember before cutting anything to length, whether it is timber, metal or stone, is the old adage – 'measure twice and cut once'.

Leaving the job

At the end of the day clean off tools – particularly those that have been used for concreting or bricklaying – before the cement dries hard. Open bags should be placed into a bin liner and brought into a shed or porch for the night. Protect concrete footings and walls built during the day from rain with plastic sheets as well as unopened bags of cement. It's also good practice to cover stacked bricks and blocks because mortar sticks to them more readily when they are dry. Cordon off any foundations with brightly coloured marker tape or cover over with timber boards and lock away tools and equipment.

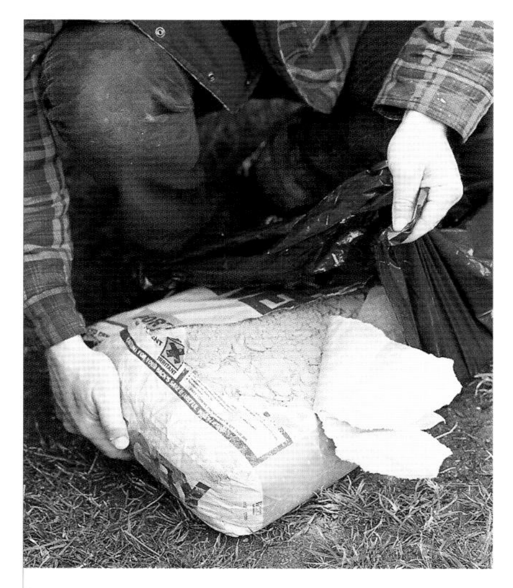

Place open bags of cement in bin liners.

Cordon off foundations with marker tape.

tools and EQUIPMENT

With the right tools, you're halfway there to getting the job done quickly and well. Some tools, such as spades, are a good investment as they are sure to be used time and again while others can be hired in for specific jobs. The tools have been split into categories: groundwork, masonry and bricklaying, and carpentry plus a section with the tools most economical to hire.

Groundwork tools

Sledgehammer This long-handled and weighty hammer is a crude but very effective tool. Its uses range from simple demolition to driving fence spikes into the ground and tamping concrete around the base of posts.

Ground marking paint A water-based aerosol paint for marking out plans and fence lines on the ground. A good aid for visualizing designs before starting work.

Bamboo canes Useful for setting out the features in a garden plan before construction starts.

Mattock This looks like a pick axe and can be used for digging, but it has a flat blade, which is perfect for scooping soil from trenches. It also has one blade, which is useful for chopping through old roots.

Measuring tape This is useful for garden surveying and speeding up marking out a design on the ground.

Fencing bar An iron bar used for making holes in the ground and breaking through buried stones.

Wheelbarrow An essential piece of kit used for all construction. Choose a model with a pneumatic tyre and a metal bucket. The place to buy is a builders' merchant, as the barrows stocked by garden centres are often too weak for construction work.

Masonry and bricklaying tools

Bolster A steel chisel with a wide, blunt blade for cutting bricks, concrete blocks and stone.

Builder's line A strong woven line for marking out levels when laying bricks or for the tops of fence posts. It can be tensioned to make straight lines.

Club hammer A heavy hammer for demolition and for driving a bolster when cutting bricks.

Level A tool for all fence and wall construction enabling them to be built perfectly upright. There are long ones for finding horizontal lines over a wide area, short ones for quick reading and working in confined spaces, and 90° levels with two sets of bubbles used for positioning over the corner of a fence post to indicate if it leans to the left or to the right or forward to back.

Builders' pins These are pointed metal pegs that can be driven between bricks or into the ground for tying off a builders' line.

Pointing trowel This is a small triangular-shaped trowel used for smoothing the normal joints of brick work.

Bucket Essential for accurately measuring quantities of sand and cement by volume, tipping water and hand washing tools clean at the end of each day.

Mortar board A mortar board for brick or block laying is usually made from a square piece of plywood approximately 60 x 60cm (2 x 2ft). It acts as a place to pile mortar within reaching distance of where you are working and forms a convenient flat surface to load the trowel from.

Storey rod A gauge made from an off-cut of wood that is used to check that mortar joints in a wall are the correct depth. It is particularly useful when it comes to building walls with two skins because it helps to keep their joints at the same height as they are built.

Carpentry tools

Beetle A crude-looking rustic mallet, traditionally carved from the branch of an elm tree. Bespoke tools such as these are no longer commonplace but are a pleasure to use as they can be weighted perfectly for their purpose and the person using them.

Chisel Available in various sizes, chisels are used for cutting and squaring timber joints. For fencing joints, a 20mm (¾in) blade is fine. Keep the blade sharp and work with a wooden mallet – metal ones are hard to use accurately and will crack the handle.

Circular saw The ideal tool for cross-cutting timber to length and for cutting planks into strips. It comes with a metal guide bar (fence), which clips over the edge of the plank, keeping the blade straight. This saw is battery-powered, so you can use it away from a source of electricity, but it is less powerful. If you are cutting thick timber with access to electricity, hire an electric model.

Jigsaw A useful electric saw for cutting curved and straight lines. It comes with interchangeable blades for sawing timber, plastic and sheet metal. The trick to accurate cutting with a jigsaw is to look over its top at the blade while working. Doing this enables you to guide the saw more easily and adjust its position if it strays from a line.

Mallet A wooden hammering tool for knocking timber joints and fence posts into position without marking them and for driving wood chisels.

Panel saw An all-purpose saw for cutting timber to length.

Workbench Choose a model with a large top and clamps for holding materials while you work.

Residual Current Device (RCD) Sometimes known as a circuit breaker, an RCD is an essential piece of safety equipment for use with all electrical power tools. It can turn off the supply of electricity if it detects that the power cable has been cut or the tool developed a fault, thus reducing the risk of electrocution. The power tool is simply plugged into the RCD, which in turn is plugged into an electrical socket.

Router A power-tool with a spinning blade, used for bevelling the edges of timber boards. Different blades can be used to achieve a range of finishes.

Surform A useful tool used for planing timber. It has a blade reminiscent of a cheese grater – ideal for removing sharp edges from timber boards.
Try square This is a set square that is used for woodworking.

Hire equipment

Any tool can be hired, from screwdrivers up to tractor-mounted excavators, rented out on a daily rate. To save money, only hire tools as you need them and choose a hire firm that will deliver and collect the tools when you have finished with them. When hiring equipment with a petrol engine, such as a cement mixer or auger, check whether fuel is supplied and, if you don't own one already, hire a fuel can to keep it topped up.

All mechanical hire equipment comes with safety instructions and it is your responsibility to read them. But, safety equipment such as protective goggles, ear defenders and dust masks are often supplied separately.

Although hiring tools will make any job more expensive, they will save time and will reduce tedious or back-breaking work such as digging holes for fence posts or foundations.
Cement mixer Mixing concrete and cement by hand is a back-breaking job that a mechanical mixer will do for you. Always hire an electric mixer where there is a power supply as they are quieter than petrol models and easier to start.

Fencing spoons An ingenious long-handled excavating tool for digging deep, steep-sided holes for fence posts. Inexpensive to hire and a real time saver.

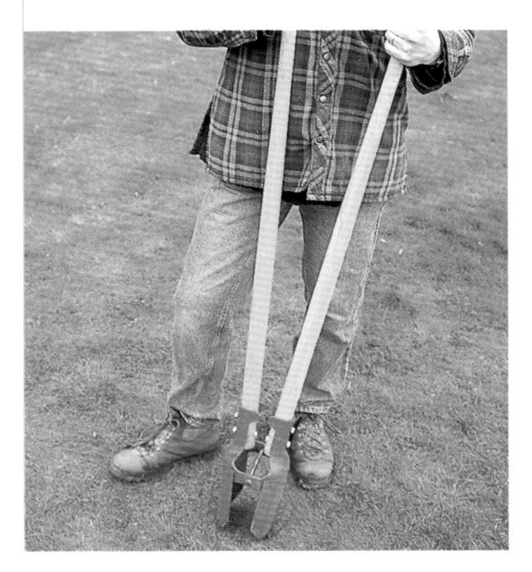

Paint sprayer An economical tool to hire that will save hours of brushwork (days even if you're painting trellis) and reduce the amount of paint you use. Always wear a mask.

Petrol auger The fastest way to dig a line of holes for fence posts is with one of these. As the blade turns it screws into the ground pushing out the soil. You have to be strong to use one alone, but most can be operated by two people.

Trenching spade A reinforced spade with a flat blade for digging straight-sided holes and foundations. Hire if your plans require lots of digging.

Turf remover Worth hiring if you are creating borders next to a boundary or making over a whole garden. This machine will save you the blisters and time it takes to cut away grass by hand.

Equipment

Decorative nails Thick iron nails with ornamental heads, which give a stud-work finish to gates. They can be bought in various lengths and rust proofed to prevent black stains from developing as the iron reacts to the timber. Because they have wide shanks, they need pilot holes to prevent the timber from splitting. To clamp lengths of timber together, use long nails and bend ends over.

Drainage pipe 100mm (4in) This collects water through holes in its side. It is laid underground in a bed of gravel or sulphate-free hardcore (sulphate salts would clog it up), and connects to a land drain. To carry water effectively, drainage pipes must be laid with a slope of 1cm for every 70cm in length.

Fencing spikes These are metal sockets for fixing fence posts. As well as spikes for hammering into soil, they can have plates or wings for bolting/setting in concrete and short wedge-shaped spikes, which are hammered down the sides of broken fence posts to repair them.

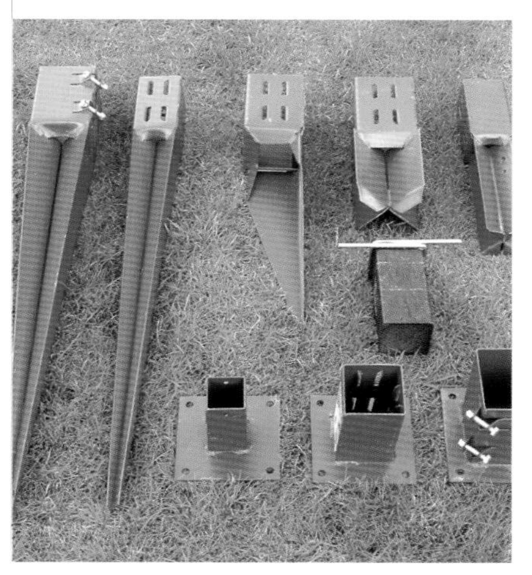

Hinges and latches There are many different types on the market and your choice will depend on whether you want them to be discrete or decorative. For outdoor use, though, always go for those protected with rustproof paint.

Fence spike driving tool A protective plastic block that is inserted into the socket of the fence spike while it is driven into the ground.

Staples C-shaped nails used for fixing wires and screen cladding to fences. Always choose galvanized staples as they won't rust.

Brick ties Loops or lengths of curved galvanized wire that are laid between courses and used to lock walls made of two independent skins of brick or block-work together.

Using these tool lists

To save repetitive lists of tools appearing at the end of each project, only the necessary categories of equipment (masonry and bricklaying, for example) have been recorded. If any item from another section is also required to complete the project, it is listed individually. Any necessary hire equipment is also shown.

walls

planning for walls

When you visit the gardens of a stately home, inevitably many of the garden rooms are enclosed by venerable old walls, the details of the mortar and the patterns of the brick like laughter lines on a characterful face. Long-lasting and solid, walls impart a feeling of permanence and reassurance, regardless of whether the place is new or ancient.

Function and style This book concentrates on low walls as they are most manageable for DIY work and don't stray into the area that requires planning permission. Consequently, these walls are most suited to either front gardens or low internal boundaries around patios and sunken gardens. Many also make good retaining walls, suitable for creating terraces and level areas on sloping sites, and can double up as seating.

The materials used for walls are many, from traditional bricks, stone and timber to more modern reclaimed railway sleepers and gabions. Which you use, depends on budget, ability and the style that suits you and your space. The larger the basic element of the wall, the quicker it is and the less skill it takes to build. However, you must bear in mind that building with large units, like sleepers, is often a two-person job. And you may want to spend more time later on detailing, such as coping or planting. The other advantage is that larger units are cheaper.

On the other hand, small units are far more versatile for creating curved and serpentine boundaries which look good as internal screens, because they disguise the perimeter and lead your eye into the centre of the garden.

Design choices Walls are either formal or informal in appearance, depending on the material used in their construction and finish. At one end of the scale, a smooth rendered wall coated with a glossy paint has a crisp man-made look. At the other extreme, a random stacked stone wall with plants cascading from between the rocks presents a much softer, natural face. In between, mixing old and new, are adaptable materials, such as gabions.

Stone, when laid in definite courses, can look architectural enough to blend with buildings while at the same time soft

Stone wall of various heights.

A wall to harmonize with the house.

Old style garden wall.

Soil-filled dry stone wall.

One of the most common uses for walls is to hold back soil (top left). Such walls make excellent seats and shelves for pots of plants. Low walls also create interesting internal divides separating a path from a gravel garden or retaining the soil adjacent to a stepped path (top right and above).

Country meets classical – the undulating face of this dry stacked stone wall contrasts beautifully with the straight-edged pier.

enough to harmonize with plantings of the garden as a whole. A soil-filled dry stone wall is more like a hedge than a wall, because of the way it becomes festooned with plants.

Rendered and brick walls both blend effortlessly with houses, but depending on the finish and colour of the brick or render, can enhance a cottage-garden, city or even Mediterranean theme. Plus there are plenty of home-spun details that give a wall a personal character, such as incorporating bottle ends during construction.

A low wall is the strongest of any physical enclosure, even if it is no more than (1m) 3ft high. This is especially the case around a patio because you are normally sitting down, and anything solid that's higher could make the space feel oppressive. But that's not to stop you placing lighter screens on top of the wall, for example, picket fencing, or clouds of plants.

Types of wall

Brick – there are thousands of different types of brick and various patterns to lay them. Warm and established in character, brick works well near houses or outbuildings. There are also special bricks for coping and corners.

Rendered – render can give an ugly wall a new lease of life, or give an economically-made concrete block wall an expensive, up-to-the-minute finish. It's a chameleon, fitting neatly with cottage-gardens, city spaces and sun-baked Moroccan-style courtyards. Leave rough for a mud wall look, smooth for a crisp urban finish, or undulate the surface to replicate the appearance of the rendered stone walls of a Moroccan villa.

Sleeper – sleepers are becoming more and more popular, not just for walls, but also for steps and paths. They are straightforward to lay and for their warm, chunky look, are adaptable to all styles of gardens.

Stone – sandstone and limestone are the most common types used for walling. They can be bought as random or 'dressed' boulders, ie shaped into blocks. Dressed stone creates a wall with regimented courses and is easier to lay, while random stone has a more rustic appearance, unless carefully napped and put together like a jigsaw, for an Oriental feel.

Gabions – gabions have long been used to shore up banks and the sides of watercourses. But since metal has become more popular in a garden setting, gabions have been given a new spin with more interesting types and colours of stone, such as slate and dressed York stone.

This rendered concrete block wall (above left), painted in warm terracotta is the perfect backdrop to the Cyprus and citrus trees in this Mediterranean themed garden. The concrete block raised pond (above right) is softened with render and painted vibrant red. It has an almost plastic look and makes a lively contrast to the soft planting at its base and the curly-leaved sedge in the water.

Rammed earth wall.

Gabion wall.

Contoured paving stone.

Heavy duty stacked wall sleeper.

sleeper WALL

Railway sleepers have a myriad of uses in the garden, and make good-looking low walls that are quick to build. Their wood is warm and chunky, and when used for a retaining wall it doubles up as a seat and somewhere to display pots of flowers.

1. Mark out the position of the sleeper wall and excavate roughly 300mm (12in) of soil from the bank to give you room to work behind. Level and firm the ground before laying the bottom course of sleepers on edge. The sleepers then act as a guide helping you to locate the positions of the 50 x 50mm (2 x 2in) timber pegs that support them. Hammer one peg into the soil every metre (3ft) driving it in until it is about 75mm (3in) lower than the finished height of the wall. (When cutting pegs to length, ensure that the points on their ends are even otherwise they will tilt when driven into the ground.)

2. Where the sleepers meet at a corner, mark and cut them with a saw so that they fit perfectly together. To ensure that your cuts are straight, mark right around the sleeper to guide you as you saw through the timber.

MATERIALS

New sleepers

500mm (20in) tanalized 50 x 50mm (2 x 2in) timber pegs

100mm (4in) screws

TOOLS

Masonry and bricklaying tools

Drill/driver

1 Having laid the first course of sleepers on edge and back-filled with soil, hammer pegs behind them as a support.

2 Next mark and cut the sleepers that meet at a corner. Doing this gives a much neater finish than a butt-join.

KNOW YOUR MATERIALS

Because reclaimed railway sleepers are impregnated with tar, they are unsuitable for use as seats or any place where you will brush against them and pick up the tar on your clothes. For this reason it is much better to buy new sleepers that are made from untreated larch or pine, because they are clean and can either be painted to match the colour scheme in your garden or left to turn sun-bleached white, as seen in this project. If you do choose to use reclaimed sleepers, always buy grade 1 sleepers (they are graded 1–3 according to their condition). Avoid any with gummy patches of tar and cover their tops with strips of decking.

***3** Once the sleepers are in position, drive a screw through the back of each peg into the sleepers. Finally, back-fill with soil and plant.*

As you stack the sleepers back in position, make sure the joints between the second course of sleepers don't overlap with the first, so that the two courses lock together.

3 With the sleepers back in their final position, check that they are upright with a spirit level and fix them in place with 100mm (4in) screws driven through the back of each peg into the sleepers. Back-fill with soil and plant behind the wall. Then lay decking or gravel at its base.

Drainage

Joints in sleeper walls aren't sealed and allow excess water in the soil behind them to escape. Therefore they don't need extra drainage holes or pipes to take the water away.

Tall retaining walls

For walls above knee height, increase width and strength by laying the sleepers on their sides. Walls taller than 1m (3ft) should have a 15° lean into the soil behind. Drill holes through sleepers and link with mild steel rods.

soil-filled STONE WALL

A stone wall is the ultimate bespoke boundary as every single rock is unique and no two people would lay them in the same way. As well as the warmth and inherent charm of the stone, more practically speaking you cannot get a more solid boundary than this.

1 This wall differs from the rustic stone walls used for stock enclosure in places like Dartmoor or Cumbria as soil is packed into its centre. This means plants can root into it, creating a colourful garden feature as well as a boundary.

Mark out the base of the wall on the ground using sand or ground marking paint. Make the width 600mm (24in) and for strength give it a curved or serpentine shape. Then use a spade to dig out the top 150mm (6in) of soil to give you a firm even base to build from. Pile the soil close by for use later on.

2 Before building, organize your working area by laying out as many stones as space allows so that you can quickly pick and choose between them. The message is that once a stone is picked up, it should never be put down unless it's in the wall. Although this is sound advice, you

MATERIALS

- Dressed York stone blocks
- Topsoil
- Plants
- Leaky/micro irrigation hose

TOOLS

- Masonry and bricklaying tools
- Spade
- Length of wood
- Brick hammer

1 Having decided upon the shape and size of your wall, mark out the base on the ground and dig out 150mm (6in) of soil.

2 Lay the first course of stones along both edges of the footing, fitting them snugly together.

KNOW YOUR MATERIALS

There is an old saying 'stone for walls doesn't travel far' that is as true today as it ever was because the cost of haulage is high. So, when it comes to choosing stone, always source it locally to save money and to ensure that it blends with your surroundings. This is less of an issue if you live in a city where its use in residential buildings is limited, but, if you do have stone in your garden already, try and match the wall with it, otherwise there is a danger that your garden will become a hotchpotch of different materials that lack harmony. Always ask your supplier to help quantify how much stone you'll need, as the amount will vary according to the size and type of stone used.

brick and RENDER

The vivid paint colours in modern garden designs such as Mediterranean blue and earthy ochre have given the rendered wall a new lease of life. They are once again held in regard for their smart, flawless finish and yet they are surprisingly easy to build.

1 Use ground marking paint to mark out the position of the wall on the soil and lay the foundations (see pages 18–21 for details on specification). Screed the surface of the concrete flat with a length of timber and allow at least two days drying time before building to allow the concrete to harden fully.

2 Organize your building area by stacking blocks within easy reach of the face of the wall and set a timber mortar board on a few blocks next to where you're starting. If you are building a curved wall (like the one pictured right), cut some of the blocks in half by sitting them on soft ground and striking them with a club hammer and bolster right around where you want to make the cut. Making the blocks smaller in this way allows you to create a smoother arc on the curve.

MATERIALS

- High density concrete blocks
- Ballast
- Cement
- Soft sand
- 12mm (½in) plastic pipe for weep holes
- Bitumastic sealant
- Plastic damp-proof membrane

TOOLS

- Groundwork tools
- Masonry and bricklaying tools
- Metal and plastic float
- Timber mortar board

1 Once you have marked the position of the wall on the ground, lay the foundations. Use timber to screed the surface of the concrete flat.

2 Use a club hammer and bolster to cut some blocks in half. Having smaller blocks allows yo to create a smoother arc on the curve.

KNOW YOUR MATERIALS

Render is tremendously versatile and can be used to achieve dozens of effects. Smoothed and painted, it can have all the shine of plastic, or if left rough with the lines of the float still showing, it has the appearance of rammed soil. For a weathered stone effect, smooth the render into gentle undulations and coat with earthy coloured paint. The coping also affects the look. Bricks and polished paving stones are crisp and clean, while timber decking creates a seaside feel. For a jungle look, round the render over the top of the wall, creating the illusion that the wall is made from mud. Give it a lick of zingy ginger paint and plant large-leaved palms and grasses behind.

brick WALL

This wall is warm on the eye and to the touch, and it holds back the soil and nurtures the plants in its shelter. The curve leads up a flight of steps, while its top makes the ideal ad hoc seat for parties. Unfortunately, having a retaining wall built for you can be expensive. This project combined with the information in the techniques section, tells you all you need to know to do it yourself and how to save money on materials.

1 Mark out and excavate the foundation for the wall using a line attached to a cane to scribe the arc of the wall. Then, pour concrete into the foundation, allowing a gap of at least two courses between the top of the foundation and the soil level. This is to make space for plants or paving. When you are building a wall into a bank, step the foundation to reduce the number of bricks needed to reach soil level. To build a flight of steps into the bank, you will need retaining walls to hold the soil from their sides as well as along the face of the bank. To build a stepped foundation, peg a piece of timber overlapping the lower foundation by at least 450mm (18in). The rise of the step must equate to the height of the course (that is, one or two bricks plus their mortar joint), or it will be difficult to marry the wall above and below the step.

MATERIALS

Ballast and building sand
Chalk
Cement
Bricks
High density concrete blocks
Brick ties
Bamboo cane
Stone effect concrete paving slabs

TOOLS

Groundwork tools
Masonry and bricklaying tools
Board to lay mortar on

1 Smooth over the surface of the foundations using a trowel. Leave at least two days for the concrete to dry before starting construction.

2 Lay blocks along the back face of the straight part of the wall, starting with the end blocks.

KNOW YOUR MATERIALS

To save time and money, concrete blocks can be used to build up the back of the wall, hidden behind stretcher bond face bricks. Concrete blocks and bricks are deliberately proportioned for use together and a single course of concrete blocks is equal in height to three courses of bricks. When the two courses are at the same level (ie, every 3, 6, 9 bricks), the two can be joined with brick ties. These are galvanized S-shaped rods, which are bedded into the mortar every 900mm (3ft) along the wall. Alternatively, build the out-of-sight part of the wall using commons. These are bricks that have an uneven colour and texture, and a low price tag.

fences

planning for fences

Fences have the important function of demarcation, but they don't need to be boring. Not only are there lots of different types of fences, but many variations in style that each can adopt. Timber is the most common type of garden boundary. It is infinitely versatile, weathers well and looks natural in a garden setting. Whether made from panels or slats of wood, it creates a neat, rhythmical line that complements the softer, less formal shape of borders.

Function and style Timber has been used in gardens for thousands of years, because it is easy to work with, long-lasting and integrates with the garden as it ages. Depending on the type of fence, wood lends itself to large perimeter boundaries or lighter internal divides. Truly adaptable, it can be a defence against trespassers or an enclosure to keep children in, or an inviting front garden picket that beckons visitors with a glimpse of the garden.

The main choice is whether to make fences from scratch, cutting timber posts and planks exactly to your own design, or to buy in simpler panel form. There are advantages to each – a home-made version will be perfectly customized to your garden and taste, whereas panel fences are quicker and simpler to erect.

The style is often dictated by the construction methods, for example whether you are using metal brackets or linking the wood with more rustic interlocking mortice joints. The more craft that goes into the fence, the more beautiful it can be. If you are looking for an opportunity for creativity, go for a picket fence. There are infinite possibilities for the shape of the uprights, from Gothic points to arrowheads, as well as any new design of your own.

Design choices One of the first questions you should ask is whether the fence is to be a physical enclosure, so you can see through it or over it but it stops you in your tracks, or a visual enclosure, creating a total screen from the outside world. For example, a picket fence or a low post and rail offers physical enclosure without blocking views or lowering light levels, unlike a close board fence.

In a countryside setting there are often opportunities for incorporating the surrounding landscape into the garden, in which case you want a fence that subtly demarcates your

A timber pole divide.

Close board fence.

Living willow fence.

Rustic pole fence.

Climbing plants can really spruce up a fence (top left), their foliage blending the timber with the garden. If it is contrast you're after, paint effects, such as black wood stain with acid green paint (top right) make a zingy colour combination. For decoration (above), an arrow-topped picket fence combined with an ornamental arch create a façade with style.

Heavy oak post and rail fences are charming and long lasting – useful for both perimeter and internal divides.

land without detracting from the view. A post and rail is not only see-through but the hewn chestnut rails appear as if they have just been cut from the surrounding trees. On the other hand, in an exposed area or a rural setting you may want a boundary that makes you feel safe and says 'keep out' while providing seclusion, and the best option for this is a close board fence.

Both fences could work as well in a city or suburban environment, but here there are more opportunities for modern twists with woodstains or claddings. Timber boundaries will always be in vogue because of the way they allow you to ring the changes, whether with a fresh paint or by tying in with decking for a modern, Scandinavian look. Dripping with roses and clematis, and allowed to bleach in the sun, they can look old-fashioned or be planed and painted to give a modern, metallic finish.

Types of fencing

Panel – this is probably the most ubiquitous type of fence, popularly sold in 1.8 x 1.8m (6 x 6ft) units that are economical to buy and fairly simple to construct, because they go up in 1.8m (6ft) chunks and are held in the ground by fence posts on either side. The more you pay, the better the timber, construction and the detailing of the panel. Bottom of the range larch panels tend to become warped over time and really need to be clothed and hidden by plants. You have a choice of wood or concrete gravel boards and posts.

Hit-and-miss – when viewed straight on, this double-faced fence appears solid, but when looked at from the side, you notice it has gaps to allow the breeze to filter through it, making it ideal for a windy, exposed situation.

Post and rail – this is a very simple enclosure and depending on the wood used and the finish, it can have a modern or country look. It can be charming when the flowerheads of low perennials poke through the gaps.

Close board – the effect is like a well-made panel fence, but in fact, it's constructed from individual planks of timber nailed to a post and rail frame. Because it's made from separate timbers, it's easy to modify, say to avoid the branches of a tree or to follow curved or sloping ground. Like a panel fence it is easily painted and embellished with decorative finials and capping rails.

Picket – these have bags of charm because they are architectural enough to pick up details in houses, but open and airy enough to allow plants to grow through. Most often used for front gardens, but perhaps under-used as internal divides, such as around a vegetable patch.

The downside of solid fences is that they block out light, making the conditions on their lea side cold and shady. Where possible, it is much better to use fences with gaps between their spars, such as this hit and miss palisade (top left) or diamond-crossed fencing (top right). In more clement growing conditions, plants will happily fill the gaps and even billow through their sides.

Arrowhead picket.

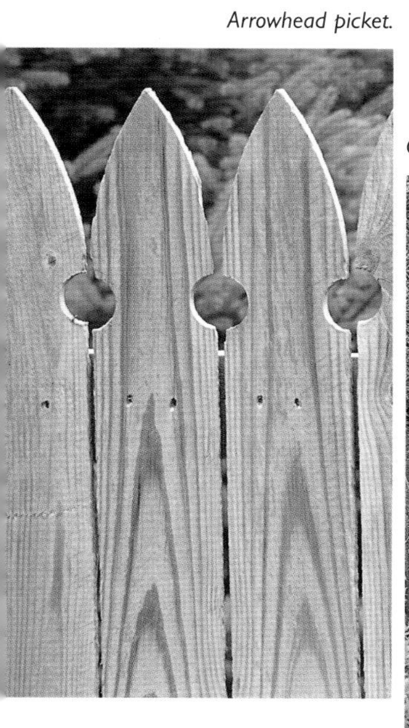

Chestnut pole palisade.

Hexagon picket.

Wattle hurdle.

post and RAIL

A split chestnut post and rail fence creates a rustic-looking divide that harmonizes with meadow areas, and cottage-style gardens. The twisted honey-coloured wood makes a see-through frame for borders in winter that gradually fills with flowering plants through the summer.

1 The height of the posts and the length of the rails depend on the location of the boundary. In a large garden cutting down the posts and rails isn't necessary. However, in most gardens it is a good idea to cut down the posts and rails using a panel saw into 1.2m (4ft) lengths, to produce a scaled down version. To mark the positions of the rails on the fence posts, mock up the fence flat on the ground, moving the rails up and down until they look right. I made the centre of the rails 160mm (6½in) and 500mm (20in) down from the top of the fence post. Make the joints for the rails about 75mm (3in) long and 25mm (1in) wide, drilling out as much wood as possible before chiselling them square.

2 Cut the rails to length if necessary and sharpen their ends using a billhook or axe (resting them over a block

MATERIALS

1.8m (6ft) chestnut posts

TOOLS

Carpentry tools

Masonry and bricklaying tools

Billhook or axe

Drill

1 Make mortice joints in the posts by first drilling out as much wood as possible and removing the rest with a chisel.

***2** Once the rails have been cut to length, rest them on a block of timber or a tree stump an use a billhook or an axe to sharpen their ends*

KNOW YOUR MATERIALS

The most common use for chestnut fence spikes are as supports for economical temporary cordon fences around building sites. But it is as post and rail fences that chestnut excels. This is due to the twisted and curved nature of the timber which creates a boundary with a soft, wavy outline. Often the cheapest way to buy is from a woodland or wildlife trust, although they are available in 1.8m (6ft) lengths from builders' merchants. When you buy, handpick the lengths yourself choosing the widest for the posts and narrower lengths for the rails. Alternatively, buy pre-morticed square 750mm (30in) posts to create a more formal fence.

Use a sledgehammer to drive the posts into ne ground, having hooked the rails between he two posts.

of timber or a tree stump is the easiest way to do this). Overlap inside the fence posts making what's called a 'scarf joint'. This gives the rail a neat finish – especially if you sharpen the opposite side of each end as shown. Also sharpen the ends of the post into points.

3 Use a sledgehammer to drive the first post into the ground, checking by eye that it is upright. Take another post, position it and hook rails between the two. They don't need to be tight, as they will be pushed into the joints as you hammer the second post into the ground. Repeat the process right along the fence run. An option at each end is to attach two rails, angling them down from the fence into the soil to give extra support.

Chestnut posts have a remarkable ability to resist the weather and won't rot in above-ground positions for decades. However, it is wise to give the posts extra protection and the best way of doing this is to dip their bases in wood preservative before hammering them into the ground.

post and PANEL

Painted in gentle, hazy blue, this line of dome-topped panel fencing makes the perfect backdrop to a fresh, clean-looking garden. Its straight, crisp lines echo those of the deck and contrast beautifully with the pebbles and large, tropical palms.

1 Most panels have been treated with a timber preservative as part of their manufacture but because the colours are often so lurid, you'll need to paint them anyway. It is a good idea to do this before you build the fence, as it is easier to get into nooks and crannies on both sides without having to step on your own, or neighbours' borders. It also allows you to catch the drips of paint that run from one side of the fence to the other.

2 Run a taut string along the ground to mark out the front of the fence and level out any undulations in the ground. This is necessary because panel fences, particularly those with domed or concave tops, look best when they are all level. If you are building your fence on a slope and have a slight rise along your fence line, you can raise the height of the fence at the bottom of the slope by fixing an

MATERIALS

Dome-topped fence panels

Paint

Pressure-treated 100mm (4in) wooden post and ball-shaped caps

Fence spikes

1.8m (6ft) gravel boards

380mm (15in) wooden pegs

TOOLS

Masonry and bricklaying tools

Fence post driver

Drill driver

1 Start by painting the panels before erecting them, so that you can get into all the nooks and crannies with ease.

2 Having marked out the front of the fence and levelled the ground, hammer in the first fence spike, making sure it is upright.

KNOW YOUR MATERIALS

There are hundreds of different styles of panel fence, ranging from the ubiquitous larch to bamboo and willow panels held in a timber frame. The rule is the more you pay, the more robust the panels will be, and the more thought and time will have gone into their detailing and design. The panels used in this project are made up of two lines of overlapping boards with a 20mm (¾in) gap between them. The gap is small enough to maintain privacy but still allows air to filter through the fence, reducing turbulence on its lea side and buffeting when wind speeds are high (for further information see page 10). For an alternative look, use square or concave-topped panels.

close board FENCING

The close board fence combines elegant, regimented lines with strength and rhythm, created by the repeated overlapping boards and arris rails. It is structurally very strong, and it will take the weight of large climbers and trained fruit trees.

1 The ends of each arris rail have a notch of wood removed from them that corresponds to a similar notch cut in the posts, creating a half-lap joint. This joint gives the fence extra strength and brings the face of the arris rails in line with the face of the posts, so that the feather-edge boards form one continuous line running the length of the fence. To create the notch in the arris rails, lay them with their widest face down and make a saw cut 50mm (2in) in from the ends and 25mm (¾in) deep. Then, starting from the end of the arris, chisel back to the saw cut, removing the uppermost triangle of wood. Chiseling can be made easier and more accurate by making two or three extra saw cuts in from the end.

2 To make the notch in the fence posts, first mark in pencil the tops and bottoms of the arris rails. The top rail should be 300mm (12in) from the top of the post, the bottom

MATERIALS

Triangular arris rail

100mm (4in) wide posts and 2.5m (8ft) long feather-edge boards

75mm (3in) galvanized nails

Cement and hardcore

150mm (6in) gravel boards

50mm (2in) nails

Post caps and cover strips

TOOLS

Carpentry tools

Groundwork tools

Masonry and bricklaying tools

1 Once you have made a saw cut in the arris rail, chisel back to the cut removing the uppermost triangle of wood.

2 Having marked the tops and bottoms of the arris rails onto the post and used a circular saw to cut along the lines, chisel out the wood

KNOW YOUR MATERIALS

A close board fence consists of feather-edge boards nailed to horizontal lengths of timber called arris rails, which in turn are fixed to fence posts. As all of the components fit together like a kit, the height of the fence and the distribution of the fence posts can be tweaked to avoid obstacles such as tree roots and branches, or to enclose difficult spaces. Usually though, the posts are set at 2.5m (8ft) centres because the arris rails are sold in 5m (16ft) lengths and cutting them in half makes them easy to handle and avoids waste. There are two types of arris rail, triangular (used here) and square with a bevelled top. Of the two, the triangular shape has more graceful lines.

picket FENCE

A walk down any country lane will take you past cottages fronted by charming picket fences, with climbers spun through the top and flowers poking their heads between the palisade. The look need never be clichéd because picket has such potential for whimsical detail that accentuates the personality of its home and owner.

MATERIALS

14 x 70mm (¾ x 2½in) planed timber for the pickets

Paint

75mm (3in) fence posts

Concrete

Batten braces

Screws

Treated timber

21 x 70mm (⅞ x 2¾in) planed timber for the arris rails

Height gauge and spacer

Decorative caps

TOOLS

Jigsaw

Surform/sander/grinder/abrasive paper

Spirit level

Handsaw

Drill driver

1 Sketch out designs that will go with your house. When you've decided which is the most appropriate, make a template from an off-cut of wood to aid marking out. As well as the shape of the top, consider the size of the gap between them and decide how far apart the pickets need to be to look their best. If the space is wider than the width of the timber it will look gappy, so modify your design until it you think it looks good, with a space somewhere between two-thirds and the full width of the timber.

2 Cut the timber for the pickets to length. This should be the desired height of the fence less 50mm (2in), so the base of the pickets is clear of the soil and away from rot. Draw around the template on the end of each picket and cut to shape using a jigsaw. To save time, clamp two pickets at a time to a workbench.

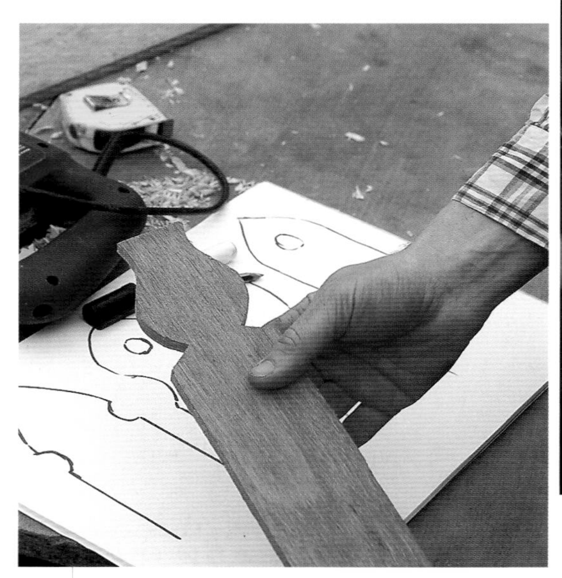

1 When you have chosen a design for your pickets, use a jigsaw to make a template from an off-cut of wood.

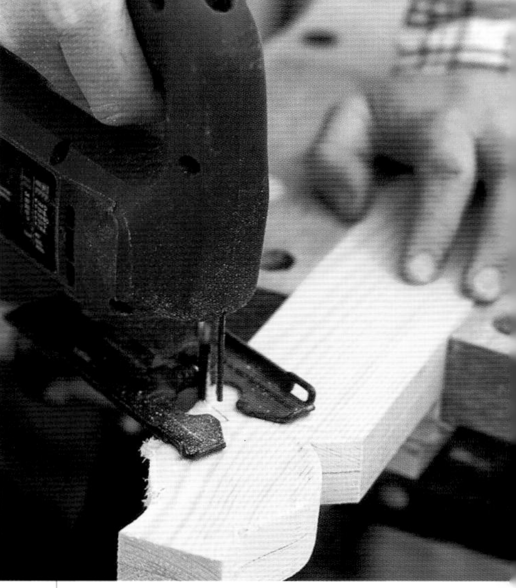

2 Having drawn around the template on each picket, clamp two to a workbench and cut to shape.

CHOOSING A DESIGN

It's worth taking time to assess the height of your fence. Too small and it can look twee, above waist-height and its elegance is lost. Between 0.5 and 1m (19½ and 39½in) is ideal, depending on the size of the garden it encloses. As for the tops, take your cue for the shape from the location, such as the house, the greenhouse or shapes of distant roofs. The timber for this fence was cut into tulips, echoing the curvy lines of the thatch roof on the cottage it surrounds and as a hint as to the owner's passion for flowers. Think about the shape of the gaps between the timbers too. Here they make wine goblet shapes, a celebratory touch.

trellis, screens and claddings

planning for trellis, screens & claddings

This chapter is devoted to masquerade – hiding the reality of ugly boundaries with dramatic embellishments, while increasing your privacy in the process. Suggestive of outdoor living, the materials are influenced by trends in interior design, which rely on the beauty of individual materials and how well they marry with a natural setting. Their appeal derives as much from the components as the way the light plays through and across their surfaces.

Function and style While the theme of creating privacy and enclosure persists, these trellis, claddings and screens have various functions. Glass gives an open-plan and airy feel to a space, and is particularly suited to small, already-enclosed gardens. It can be used as a detail within a trellis or as the screen itself. The only type of glass to use is toughened and sandblasted as it is opaque, and therefore not a danger to birds, and, of course, very strong. It's a dynamic material that reflects its surroundings and becomes more transparent in rain. At night, in the beam of a spot lamp, it glows and diffuses the light around.

The best trellis has not forgotten its classical heritage, reminiscent of Greek colonnades and Roman cloisters. Sadly, all too often it doesn't live up its promise due to cheap construction and unimaginative use. But when made well, bespoke trellis gives a romantic other-worldliness to an existing wall, and offers exciting opportunities for climbing plants and night-time lighting.

For a more instant transformation you can't beat cladding, such as those made from natural stems like split bamboo. Wired together on rolls, the bamboo can disguise an unappealing fence or enhance a theme, like a Japanese garden. It is economical and certainly much cheaper than replacing a whole fence. More sophisticated metal claddings, like copper and stainless steel, aren't for such wholesale use. Instead, they can be used as focal points, giving an ordinary boundary an artistic twist.

Temporary screens, like the summer structures that support sweet peas and runner beans, are playful and seasonal. By replacing traditional allotment materials such as bamboo canes with hazel, a plant support screen will last for a good few years. It is also a fantastic way of creating instant rooms, while waiting for permanent

Living willow lattice.

Painted trellis.

Woven willow with metal spars.

Bespoke heavy timber trellis.

The metal clad walls (above left and right) are surprisingly dynamic. Stainless steel reflects the shapes and colours in the garden that surrounds it, while mild steel turns through every shade of coral and cinnamon as it rusts. Both are modern and uncompromising in effect and are tricky to work with. In complete contrast, bamboo screens (above) are much simpler to construct and change little as they age.

Woven walls have their own character and no two are the same. Hazel hurdles are solid in appearance, and are suitable for perimeter and internal boundaries.

hedges to grow. More lasting are rusting weld mesh screens which have an urban feel and introduce spicy colours in an elemental way.

Design choices Glass and metal should be integrated with the surroundings, and this is best achieved by giving it a function, such as masking an unattractive feature or leading the eye to an entrance. Both need an anchor, such as an appropriately modern material at their base or plants that ground them, making them seem like they belong. Metal claddings can be used very subtly, for example to adorn window boxes. This approach works well because it links claddings on walls to other areas of the garden, making the decision to use the material less arbitrary. Similarly, with more traditional screens like timber trellis, linking them to other parts of the garden gives them reason. So, if it's painted, repeat the colour on timberwork elsewhere, such as on fence posts.

Types of trellis, screens and claddings Glass is expensive because it must be cut to size and toughened before you take delivery. On the positive side, all you have to do is fix it in position, so it's fairly instant to install. Sandblasted glass has two faces: a smooth side and the side that has been treated. For reflections, have the smooth side outermost or for a softer finish, display the other.

You can buy trellis for adding instant height to existing boundaries, for jazzing up walls and fences, and for giving body to freestanding arbours and pergolas. Bespoke trellis can be constructed to fit any space without any of the ugly joins that detract from shop-bought panels.

The various types of cladding include bamboo, tree heather, peeled reed and willow, each bestowing a garden with a different character. Bamboo obviously enhances an Oriental theme, but can also look quite jungly. Tree heather gives a Mediterranean feel, and peeled reed and willow are suited to a cottage-garden.

There are two main choices with stems – either to buy a dead stem that won't re-grow, or a living stem like willow, which will sprout and turn into a living screen. Hazel is more shy to root and bamboo canes, of course, cannot be expected ever to grow!

Metal is available in sheet form or mesh, and the latter is good for giving a modern twist on trellis. Copper and steel is sold by the sheet and can be worked at home with a jigsaw fitted with a metal blade, whereas stainless steel is hard to cut so should be made to order.

Trellis can be a work of art in its own right. The cladding (above left) in the style of a Mondrian painting has stained glass fixed between the bars, adding extra colour and interest. In contrast, the combination of industrial materials in a garden setting, such as stainless steel floor tiles and corrugated steel sheets (above right), shakes off their municipal associations.

Trellis as balustrade.

Light airy timber trellis.

Willow in a Japanese-style lattice.

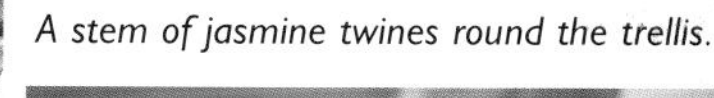

A stem of jasmine twines round the trellis.

glass SCREEN

Using glass in a garden is like bringing the indoors outside. It always looks very modern, whether combined with structural plants like phormiums and palms or with cottage-garden flowers. It's the ideal material for built-up areas, creating privacy without reducing light levels.

1 This project involves combining ready-made materials from specialists to make a screen that's unique. Decide on the measurements and number of glass panels and order frames made from 40mm (1½in) boxed steel to hold them from a blacksmith, garage or metal workshop. These should be H-shaped and wide enough to fit the glass and the clamps, plus an extra 3mm (⅛in) to make fixing the glass easier. The legs need to be at least 700mm (27½in) long to provide a deep concrete footing.

Paint the underground section of the frame with rustproof paint before putting the legs in 600mm (24in) holes in the ground and pouring a 5:1 ballast and cement mix around them. Tamp the concrete to remove any air bubbles with a length of wood and slope its surface with a trowel to shed water away from the metal. Check for level and prop in place with timber while the concrete dries.

MATERIALS

An H-shaped metal frame made from 40mm (1½in) boxed steel – this one is 2.3m (7ft) tall, and just over 1.2m (4ft) wide

Metal paint and rust proofer

Ballast

Cement

Eight metal clamps with a brushed finish

Self-tapping screws

Toughened and sandblasted 6mm (¼in) glass – this one is 1.2 x 1.5m (4 x 5ft)

TOOLS

Masonry and bricklaying tools

Drill

Allen keys (to tighten clamps)

***1** Having put the legs of the frame in holes, infill with concrete and check for level. Prop in place with timber while the concrete dries.*

***2** Once the frame is in position, paint the upper part and then attach the metal clamps to it, using self-tapping screws.*

KNOW YOUR MATERIALS

Think of a toughened glass screen like you would a car window. If it is well supported and prevented from twisting, it is extremely strong and durable. It is only vulnerable if exceptional pressure is applied to a small area, if for example, it is deliberately hit hard with a hammer. In the unlikely event of it breaking, like a car window, it shatters into tiny pieces that are unlikely to cause serious injury. Always have the glass sand blasted before it is toughened, this gives it an attractive opaque appearance and makes it visible so birds won't fly into it. Sandblasting gives one side of the glass a matt finish, while the other is glossy and reflective. The choice is yours.

***3** Lift the glass into position, resting its base on rubber stops placed on the bottom clamps. Next fit the backs on the clamps and tighten.*

2 After 48 hours, remove the timber supports and paint the upper part of the frame. Then drill evenly spaced holes for metal clamps which are fixed to the frame with self-tapping screws. Self-tapping screws work by cutting their own thread as they are tightened into the metal. They are simple to use as long as the hole they are wound into is just the right size, so either experiment on a metal off-cut with different bits or buy one to match with the screws. The clamps are made of aluminium and hold the glass in place between rubber jaws. To hold a 1.2 x 1.5m (4 x 5ft) sheet of glass you'll need eight clamps, two for the base and three up each side.

3 Lift the glass into position (this is a two-person job), resting its base on rubber stops placed on the bottom clamps. Fit the backs on the clamps and tighten. To prevent rain water getting inside the open tops of the metal frame, plug with rubber stops. And to stop unsightly mud splashes in wet weather, plant evergreens at the base or mulch with gravel.

shop-bought TRELLIS

Trellis is more than a support for climbing plants. With a little imagination, it can be transformed into a focal point, which captures the sun and shadows by day and illuminates the garden by night.

1 Painting trellis by hand is a slow and laborious business as the surface area of each panel is vast and because the timber almost always completely absorbs the first coat. It is more efficient to hire a hand-held paint sprayer which will do the job in minutes, without leaving unsightly drips down the timber. Always choose a dry still day and, to use a sprayer, water down the paint by a third, prop the trellis against a plastic sheet to catch any drift and spray evenly across each panel, paying attention to the recesses around the frame. Allow 15 minutes for the paint to dry and apply another coat. When you have finished, fill the container with warm water and spray to clean nozzle.

2 To make the trellis pillars, screw together the 0.3m (1ft) panels into three-sided boxes, using L-shaped metal brackets to hold their corners together.

MATERIALS

- Nine 1.8 x 0.3m (6 x 1ft) diamond trellis panels
- Two 1 x 1.8m (3 x 6ft) square panels
- Water-soluble paint
- Plastic sheeting
- Twelve L-shaped metal brackets
- Twelve flat metal fixing plates
- Rawl plugs
- Three low voltage 'uplights'

TOOLS

- Hire tools
- Spirit level
- Drill/driver

1 Having watered down the paint by a third, rest the trellis against the plastic sheeting and use a hand-held sprayer to paint.

2 Make the trellis pillars by screwing together the 0.3m (1ft) panels into three-sided boxes, using L-shaped brackets at the corners.

KNOW YOUR MATERIALS

To look good, trellis needs to be well made with straight spars and evenly proportioned squares. Often, shop-bought trellis falls short of these standards and although it might seem like a bargain, it never lives up to its full potential. The things that separate the good from the bad are timber quality, hole size and design. So, make sure that the finish of the wood is even and not a patchy mix of rough-sawn and smooth timber. Holes bigger than 120mm (5in) are too large and will always look out of scale and, if you're using it structurally, for example for making pillars for lighting, always opt for trellis panels with a framed edge as it increases their strength.

__3__ Screw flat metal fixing plates to the back of the trellis pillars and screw them to the wall. Use a spirit level to check they are upright.

3 Screw flat metal fixing plates to the back of the trellis pillars and screw to the wall as shown, checking that each pillar is upright with a spirit level. To fix the trellis infills between the pillars, position against the wall and drill through them to mark the plaster/brick work below. Then remove the trellis, and drill and plug the wall before placing the trellis back in position and fixing with screws.

Installing lighting

For lighting, use three low voltage 'uplights' bolted to the floor at the base of each pillar. Low voltage lights consist of a transformer that steps down the voltage from the mains electricity supply to just 12 volts, meaning that even if the wires were accidentally cut, there would be no risk of electrocution. Available as kits, you don't need a professional electrician to install them; simply position the transformer near a power socket indoors and run the wire to the lights along the base of the wall. This way the wires are hidden when the trellis is screwed in place.

bespoke TRELLIS

Bespoke trellis enables you to create an illusion of opulence and grandeur without breaking the bank. By making your own trellis you can tailor it to your garden precisely, transforming run-of-the-mill walls into classical colonnades and arches.

MATERIALS

60m (180ft) of planed 20 x 8mm (¾in x ¼in) batten

15mm (⅝in)copper tacks

1.2 x 2.4m (4 x 8ft) sheet of 12mm (½in) marine plywood

Protective wood stain

Rawl plugs

50mm (2in) screws

TOOLS

Carpentry tools

Bricklaying tools

Electric plane

Hammer

Drill with masonry bit

1 The size of the timber trellis depends on its situation. In this project 20 x 8mm (¾ x ¼in) planed batten was used as the finished trellis was situated in a yard only 5m (16ft) square. Anything bigger would have looked coarse. If you are cladding a large expanse of wall that's visible from further away, use a larger timber such as 25 x 20mm (1 x ¾in) batten. Either buy it planed or save money by removing the rough edges yourself with an electric plane. You don't need to buy treated timber, as long as the base of the trellis is above soil level and you paint it with a protective wood stain. The first thing to do when building bespoke trellis is to make your uprights by cutting twelve equal lengths of batten about 1.5m (5ft) long.

2 Cut the horizontal spars making them 150mm (6in) long and nail them to the uprights using one of the

***1** Start by making your uprights by cutting twelve equal lengths of batten, approximately 1.5m (5ft) long.*

***2** Cut the horizontal spars, making them 150mm (6in) long and nail them to the uprights using a horizontal as a spacing guide*

KNOW YOUR MATERIALS

Combining squares and diamonds gives the trellis a three-dimensional appearance. The square sections look heavier and recessed compared to the diamond panels and for this reason they look best when used as pillars, or as infill between them. Always separate the two patterns with lengths of batten or plinths (as done here) to create the impression that one sits behind or atop the other. Another trick to create a 3-D effect is to sandwich the horizontal and diamond spars between a double frame (see step 2). This means that they are held proud of the wall and it shadows to play behind them, which produces an illusion of depth.

split bamboo SCREEN

The crisp lines of a split bamboo screen can disguise all sorts of boundaries, from unattractive concrete posts and panels to boring timber fences. Bamboo screens needn't be restricted to Japanese gardens either, as they can accentuate a tropical theme wherever large-leaved plants are grown. They work well in city gardens where their strong vertical lines echo those in the surrounding urban jungle.

1. Broken, loose or rotten posts in the existing fence will need replacing first. For concrete fence posts, use a masonry drill to make and plug three holes in each – one at the top, one at the bottom and one between the two.

2. Cut a set of uprights from rough sawn timber that are 150mm (6in) lower than the finished height of the screen, and screw to the fence posts. Then measure and cut three rails for each upright and screw in position with L-shaped brackets (to compensate for any leaning posts measure and cut each rail individually). The framework isolates the screen from the fence panels, allowing them to be replaced or removed for access.

3. Unroll the bamboo and nail to the framework using staples. To ensure that the top is level, sit the unrolled

MATERIALS

2 x 5m (6½ x 16ft) split bamboo screening

50 x 50mm (2 x 2in) treated rough sawn timber

10mm (½in) staples

L-shaped brackets

25mm (1in) screws

75mm (3in) screws

(Rawl plugs if the posts are concrete)

TOOLS

Masonry drill and bits

Screwdriver

Hammer

1 Using a powerful masonry drill, make three holes in the concrete fence posts and rawl plug them.

2 Having fixed rough sawn timber uprights to the posts, cut three rails for each upright and screw them on.

KNOW YOUR MATERIALS

Bamboo screens are manufactured in Vietnam and China and since the late 1990s, new designs have become increasingly available. For an internal divide that looks good from both sides, heavy-duty, whole cane screens, wired and strung between sturdy timber posts, are just the job. Screens with twiggy tops and sideshoots, have a thatchy, less formal look. The quality of bamboo screening can vary enormously, so it is worth checking the canes before you buy.

***3** Finally, staple the bamboo onto the framework, making sure it is level by resting its base on a timber plank.*

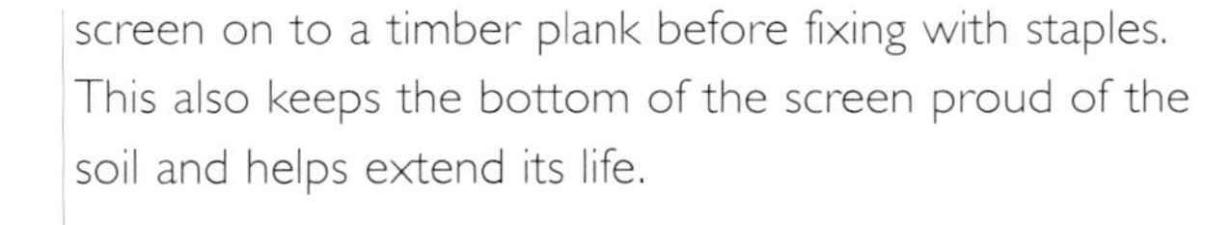

screen on to a timber plank before fixing with staples. This also keeps the bottom of the screen proud of the soil and helps extend its life.

Keeping up appearances for the neighbours

If you are raising the height of an external boundary with a screen, talk to your neighbours before starting and bear in mind that the back of the screen and the timber work that holds it in place will need to be disguised from their side. Do this, either by fixing trellis along the top of the fence or covering the visible timber work with a strip of screen. This leaves your neighbours with the existing fence topped with a neat screen coping.

Screen quality

Avoid screens that have frayed ends, slack wires or uneven spaces. A good way of judging the quality is to pick up the roll – if it feels light, the chances are that the screen is of an inferior grade and will soon deteriorate in the garden.

hazel SCREEN

This undemanding and economical hazel rod garden screen makes a perfect surround for a cut flower garden, allowing glimpses of the blooms in borders while scented sweet peas clamber up its sides.

1 Push a series of uprights into soil leaving 0.6m (2ft) spaces between them, choosing the straightest and thickest rods for this job. It's up to you whether the screen is straight, gently curved or serpentine. The base of each rod should be pressed into the soil by at least 200mm (8in). If the ground is too hard to do this by hand, make a hole with a staking bar if you've got one, or open up a slit in the ground with a spade, press the hazel rod into the opening and firm back around it. When all of the uprights are in, link them together with a horizontal hazel rod tied to each one with twine at the height you want the screen.

2 The diagonals are pushed in next, at an angle of roughly 45 degrees with 300mm (12in) spaces between them. Choose the longest lengths for the middle section of the screen and use shorter, thinner rods for the

MATERIALS

Hazel rods

Twine

TOOLS

Staking bar

Spade

Loppers

Secateurs

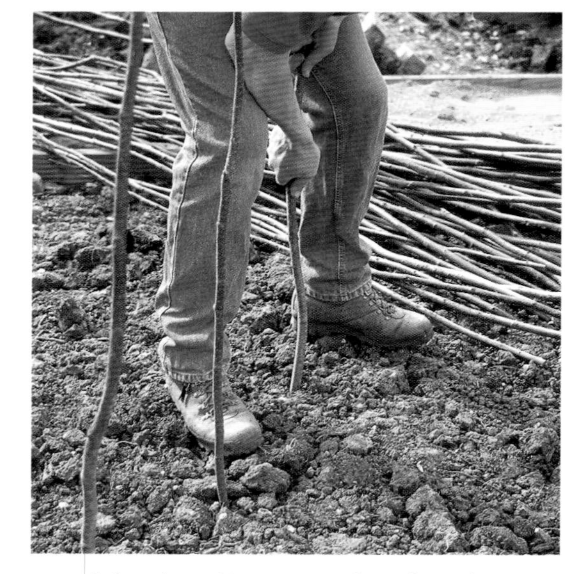

1 Start by pushing a series of uprights at least 200mm (8in) into the soil, using the straightest and thickest rods.

2 Next push the diagonals into the soil, puttin[g] the longest lengths into the central section, leaving a 300mm (12in) space between them

KNOW YOUR MATERIALS

Hazel rods have long been used in gardens for plant supports. They are cheap to buy and easy to work with, so they are perfect for building temporary screens that can be dismantled and reassembled as the mood takes you. Each rod has a useful life of four or five years after which time it becomes brittle and will need replacing. Many garden centres now supply hazel cut from local woodlands. Alternatively, it is sold by woodland and wildlife trusts who coppice it (cut it down to the ground every three to five years) to allow sunlight to reach the flowers growing on the woodland floor.

***3** Tie the diagonals to the uprights and where they cross. Twist their tops around the horizontals and tie them in.*

corners. Because the diagonals at the top right and left of the screen are above soil level, and therefore can't be pushed into the ground, they need to be tied to the uprights with twine.

3 Tie the diagonals to the uprights and where they cross. Then twist their tops around the horizontal holding them in place with twine. Alternatively, you can bind them with a few lengths of willow or simply cut them off just above the horizontal rod with loppers. Plant a row of sweet peas at the foot of the screen for scent or use other annual climbers such as nasturtium, bright yellow canary creeper (*Tropaeloum peregrinum*) or electric blue morning glory (*Ipomoea tricolor*).

Alternative materials

For an Oriental theme, use bamboo canes instead of the hazel rods, binding them together with lengths of tarred, black string. String ties can be very ornamental, especially if the same knot is used throughout.

copper CLADDING

Copper has a tremendous dynamism in a garden setting, due to the exotic blue-green patina it develops with time. It adds natural colour without risk of jarring and imbues a small space with a sense of luxury.

1 Start by cladding the wall in 12mm (½in) marine plywood to even out any irregularities in the brick or plaster work and to create a smooth surface for gluing the copper. When cladding complicated walls like this alcove, make a template out of cardboard, making sure it fits the wall perfectly. Lay the template onto the marine plywood, and draw round it and cut with a jigsaw. Fix the marine plywood to the wall by first propping it in position and drilling through every 700mm (27½in) to mark the bricks beneath. Then, remove it and drill and rawl plug the bricks, then prop it back in place and hold with screws.

2 Use the same cardboard template to mark the copper, using a marker pen to give a clear line. If there are any inaccuracies in the template they'll be visible as gaps around the marine plywood on the wall so, as you mark

MATERIALS

Cardboard

12mm (½in) marine plywood

Rawl plugs

Screws

Copper sheet (available from ironmongers)

Silicone glue or copper tacks

TOOLS

Jigsaw (sheet metal blade)

Drill

Metal file

Rubber mallet

***1** Make a template out of stiff cardboard and use it to cut out the marine plywood, which needs to be rawl plugged to the wall.*

***2** Having used the template to mark the copper, cut the copper with a jigsaw making sure the copper is well supported.*

KNOW YOUR MATERIALS

To make your copper appear old and weathered, burnish it in parts with a flame weeder or gas torch from the kitchen, the type chefs use to caramelize crème brûlée. This treatment creates dramatic dark blue clouds against the vivid copper, coloured with rainbow shades, like petrol in a puddle. Stainless steel also makes a good metal cladding. Fix it onto marine plywood in the same way as copper, except as you can't cut it yourself, measure up the area first and buy it ready-cut to size. If you prefer the distressed, seaside look of rusted metal, use mild steel sheeting. Because of its weight, bolt directly to the wall.

3 Squeeze silicone glue onto the marine plywood, then press the copper sheet back onto it. Tap it with a rubber mallet to ensure good contact.

the copper adjust the line accordingly. Cut the copper with a jigsaw fitted with a sheet metal blade. Copper is surprisingly easy to cut. Keep the blade of the jigsaw close to the side of the bench so that the copper is supported. Once cut, use a metal file to remove burrs from the edge.

3 The copper can be fixed with copper tacks or with silicone glue. Because tacks are more obtrusive it is essential that they are hammered in symmetrical straight lines or in deliberate swirls to prevent them detracting from the sheet. To do this, mark their positions before hammering home. For a smooth finish, silicone glue is best. This is available from builders' and plumbers' merchants along with the gun needed to squeeze it from the tube. Apply the glue in lines onto the marine plywood, taking particular care to coat the corners. Then press the copper sheet back onto it, tapping with a rubber mallet to ensure good contact. Prop a length of timber against the copper to hold it in place while the glue dries, which takes between three and four hours.

rusted MESH

For a modern take on trellis, steel mesh is the ideal alternative. Because it rusts, the orange complements the dark leaves of climbers like ivy, which contrive to give it Gothic good looks. Despite it rusting, it will last for years.

1 The supports for the mesh are made from boxed steel sections 25mm (¾in) in diameter. Use a hacksaw to cut to the height of the screen plus 600mm (24in) for fixing in the ground and drill holes 600mm (24in) apart right through the above ground section. Give the below ground section a coat of rustproof paint.

2 Mark the positions of the posts on the ground and dig a 300mm (12in) hole for each. Then push the posts another 300mm (12in) into the soil at the bottom of each hole, which holds them firm as you pour concrete (made from 8 parts ballast to 1 part cement) around their collars. (Use the fence post technique given on page 19 to level up the posts and ensure that they are the same height). Smooth over the top of the collars with a trowel, so that any water runs away from the posts.

MATERIALS

1.2 x 1.8m (4 x 6ft) mesh with 750 x 200mm (30 x 8in) squares

2.5m (8ft) lengths of 25mm (1in) boxed steel

Rust proofing paint

Galvanized wire

Ballast

Cement

TOOLS

Masonry and bricklaying tools

Hacksaw

Drill

Pliers

1 Cut the boxed steel to the correct length and drill holes through in order to support the mesh.

2 Dig holes for the uprights, pour concrete around them and smooth over the top with a trowel.

KNOW YOUR MATERIALS

The primary use for steel reinforcement mesh is for strengthening concrete footings and walls. It can be bought in any size from ironmongers who will build it to your specification. It is also available from builders' merchants, although the chances are that it will be delivered in 3 x 8m (10–25ft) sheets, so it will need to be cut down and possibly doubled up and wired together if the squares are larger than 150mm (6in). Cut with a hacksaw or hire a bolt cutter to do the job.

For an extra touch of detail, moon gates and arched windows can be cut into the screen and given definition by plaiting wire over the cut ends.

3 Put the mesh to in position and tie securely to the uprights using pieces of galvanized wire.

3 Tie the panels to the posts with galvanized wire looped through the holes in the posts, tightening it by twisting with pliers. Plant ivy (*Hedera*) every 300mm (12in) along the base of the screen and as it grows, train to the metal. When it is established, clip with shears in early summer to encourage it to bush out and feed with a general fertilizer.

Alternative materials

If the rusty look isn't your thing, use stainless steel or aluminium screening with aluminium box section posts. These weather to a steely grey and never rust. Ironwork can be painted, but needs to be rust free and painted with a primer first, otherwise the rust will appear after just a few months. For a more private screen with small diamond-shaped holes use sheets of barbeque mesh, which, as its name suggests, is more commonly used for cooking grills. Because the holes are small, barbeque mesh looks particularly attractive at night when back-lit with golden spotlights.

living boundaries

planning for living boundaries

This chapter has been included because you cannot talk about boundaries without at least mentioning living ones. A garden is never complete without plants and so it goes that whether it's flowers growing in a dry stone wall, climbers rambling around a gate or a hedge peeking over the top of a wooden fence, a boundary without plants is stark and cold, and never fully integrated.

Function and style You can't talk about man-made boundaries without at least touching on the planting, because the two go hand in hand. Plants embellish garden boundaries by imparting a certain dynamism to otherwise static materials. It's a two-way street, of course, because the plants benefit from the microclimate created by the boundary and the support, while the boundary can claim more seasonality as the plants flower, tint in autumn and spring into life early in the year.

Establishing Many people are more afraid of buying and growing plants than DIY, but this is a misconception based on the belief that you have to grow the plants. The plants grow themselves! The thing to worry about is giving them the right spot to grow in and getting them established. The key is to improve the soil with garden centre bought compost, well-rotted manure or homemade compost before planting. Then, make sure plants are well watered, particularly in the first summer. If your problem is which plants to choose, check out plants that are thriving in neighbours' gardens and take advice from your nearby nurseries or garden centres as they will know which species do well in the local soil.

Design choices Walls – There are three ways in which plants can be combined with walls – climbers, cascading plants for the top of retaining walls and growing plants within walls. For climbers, see fences below.

Low retaining walls make ideal falls for cascading plants, benefiting species that don't mind it dry and prefer to mound and tumble, rather than climb. Good subjects include grasses such as the red-leaved Stipa arundinacea and Carex buchanii, shrubs like Cotoneaster dammeri and

Living willow screen.

Hedge-topped fence.

Willow screen

Formal hedge.

The look of a living boundary depends on the type of plants used and how they are maintained. Regularly clipped evergreens (top left) become permanently neat surrounds, while training climbers across a trellis fence is an effective means of harnessing nature's inclination to riot. For the ultimate trained boundary, you can't beat fruit trees with their main branches espalliered (wired horizontally) for a sculptural winter framework (above).

The branches of pleached lime trees are grafted and twisted, so that in time they grow together – it is as though they are holding hands.

perennials like *Nepeta* 'Walkers Low' and many hardy cranesbill geraniums. Watering in the first year is essential for establishment. If you want plants to grow inside a wall, a leaky hose should be installed during construction and plugged into the water supply regularly.

In ready-built walls, irrigation is often impossible to install. In such cases, the best way to green them up is by sowing seed directly into soil-filled gaps. Of course, you can't put just anything in these gaps. You must choose plants that are naturally adapted to these tough conditions, such as alpines or those that happily live on steep gravel beds in the wild. Good choices from seed include *Erigeron karvinskianus*, linaria (Alpine toadflax) and thyme. By sowing direct, the plants are less likely to get a shock from the change in conditions than if they are transplanted from a pot. In time, they will begin to set seed and colonise without your intervention. This is also a good technique for establishing plants, such as Lady's mantle (*Alchemilla*), at the base of a wall or between the gaps in paving.

Fences – There are two types of climbers – self-clinging and ones that need support and both can be combined with fences. It's often said that you shouldn't put self-clinging climbers onto a fence, because of their weight, but I don't think there is a worry if the fence is well-made. Self-clinging climbers, like Virginia creeper (*Parthenocissus quinquefolia*), Boston ivy (*Parthenocissus tricuspidata*) and ivy, can look after themselves but those with tendrils, such as clematis, require a ladder of wires to help them climb. Using vine eyes to attach wires to the fence posts will allow space behind for climbers to grow and air to circulate. When planting, avoid the rain-shadow of the fence by leaving a space of 450mm (18in) between the base and the planting hole. Tilt the rootball at a 45° angle towards the support to encourage it to climb in the direction you want.

Trellis – Because trellis is more flimsy, prevent the stems growing behind the spars, as they can push it out of shape as they grow. Train the stems onto the support, by tying stems to the front with soft twine.

Hedges – Hedges are cheaper and usually more sympathetic with their surroundings than a new hard structure, but take longer to reach any height. But the two work together well, whether it's a spotted laurel and an iron railing fence in a formal front garden, or a low lavender hedge peeking through a picket. A clever combination is a yew hedge clipped into the back of a closeboard fence, so the internal screen is a green living hedge, while the outside world sees a solid timber boundary.

All living boundaries bring seasonality to a garden, but beech and hornbeam are particularly dynamic – greening up in spring and retaining russet autumn colour right through the worst of the winter. Hornbeam takes training particularly well (above left) and its main branches can be clipped into giant walls, like the hawthorne (above right).

Trellis on a panelled fence.

Half round peeled posts.

Layed hedge with ash tree.

A frost-covered beech hedge.

willow WALL

Earth and willow wands may not seem like a promising combination for a wall, but together they make a long-lasting and strong boundary. If the wall is planted with wildflowers and grasses, its sides will flower and colour with the changing seasons.

1 Mark the footprint of the wall on the ground with paint, spacing the two sides of the wall 60mm (24in) apart and connecting their ends with a gentle curve. For strength, make the sides serpentine. Then, use loppers to cut the base of the thicker willow into 1m (3ft) lengths to make the uprights, measuring at least 25mm (¾in) in diameter at their thinnest end. Push the uprights into the ground, 250–300mm (10–12in) apart, and angling the tops of the two sides together to give the sides an A-shaped profile. Having an uneven number of uprights makes weaving easier, so add an extra one, adjusting the spacing of its neighbours to fit. When you're happy with their position, hammer them firm with a wooden mallet or beetle.

2 Using single lengths of the thinner willow, weave in and out of the uprights about halfway up their sides. As you

MATERIALS

Bundles of willow 25–50mm (1–2in) for the uprights and bundles of graded willow 10–12mm (½in) in diameter for the sides

Leaky hose/micro irrigation pipe

Topsoil

Turf

TOOLS

Carpentry tools

Loppers and secateurs

Mallet or beetle

1 Having cut the lengths for the uprights, push them into the ground, spacing them 250–300mm (10–12in) apart.

2 Weave single lengths of willow in and out of the uprights halfway up their sides, and tuck the end of each length inside the wall.

KNOW YOUR MATERIALS

Willow is a fabulous building material. It is strong, malleable and so easy to work. It is available from specialist growers who supply bundles of willow mail order, but to save money it's worth looking through the telephone book for hurdle makers, thatchers or nature reserves who may point you to a cheaper local source. The time to buy is in the dormant season when the willow is cut, as summer stocks run out quickly.

The willow used for this project is the fresh green common osier (*Salix*). Also available are brightly coloured willows such as the orange *S. alba* 'Britzensis' and the black *S. daphnoides* 'Aglaia', both adding striking detail to new structures.

reach the end of each length, tuck it inside of the wall and introduce another willow length, matching the thick end of one to the thin end of the other until you've gone right around the structure twice. If you have an odd number of uprights, the second layer of willow will alternate with the first and each upright will be firmly bound inside and out. Check your weave against the photo and working round the wall, push the willow down until it is in contact with the ground.

3 The first two layers of willow rods hold the uprights steady and once they are in position, the remainder can be woven in by the handful. Take up to four or five lengths at a time and tap them down so that their thick ends are together, and weave in and out of the uprights. As before, introduce another handful when the first comes to its end, tucking any whippy bits inside the wall. Work around the wall, building up the sides in a continuous weave and making sure that each course alternates with the one below.

4 To use the willow efficiently, spread the rods in each handful out flat so that they have the widest spread. Don't worry about any small gaps, as these will be filled by grasses and flowers once the wall is established. When the sides of the wall reach half their finished height, fill between them with soil, firming it into the corners with the soles of your feet (it's much easier to do this as you go along rather than after the sides are complete).

5 Weave up to the finished height of between 700mm (27½in) and 900mm (36in), filling with soil and firming as you go and taking care to maintain the wall's A-shaped profile. (If the sides do start to splay, tie across the wall with nylon rope or thick string to hold them together.) Then, cut the tops of the uprights level with loppers and trim off any straggly tops or protruding ends using a pair of secateurs.

6 Cut the micro irrigation pipe to the length of the wall, tie a knot in one end and attach a hosepipe adaptor to the

***3** Take four or five lengths at a time and weave them through the uprights, ensuring that each course alternates with the one below.*

***4** Once the sides of the wall have reached half their height, fill between them with soil, firming it in with the soils of your feet.*

***5** Having weaved up to the finished height an filled with soil, tidy up the wall by cutting off protruding ends with secateurs.*

other. Lay the pipe on top of the wall and feed the end with the hose adaptor through the side in an inconspicuous place.

7 Next cover the hose with more soil doming it up by 100–150mm (4–6in) over the height of the sides to fill any gaps if the soil inside the wall settles. Then lay turf along the top of the wall or plant with a mixture of primroses (*Primula vulgaris*), Lady's mantle (*Alchemilla*) and cranesbill geraniums (*Geranium*).

8 To fill the pockets between each layer of willow, sow a mixture of wildflower seeds such as ox eye daisies and foxgloves. In autumn, plant bluebells and daffodils to flower the following spring. Alternatively use a mixture of herbaceous plants – in this project variegated hosta and a lemon balm (*Melissa*) sprouted from the sides after smuggling themselves in to the wall as roots mixed with the topsoil fill. They look very good and, surprisingly, are thriving in their new lofty position.

Using and caring for willow

A willow wall works both as an internal divide and around a perimeter and it looks good in any location whether urban or rural. In a country setting its soft flowery sides blend perfectly with its surroundings adding bags of cottage garden charm, while in a contemporary garden, mixed in with man-made materials, such as glass and metal, the naturalness and country craft of the wall become more apparent.

Willow has a dogged ability to survive even after the harshest treatment. So much so, that the cut branches will happily sprout new leaves even after being hammered into the ground. This tenacity makes willow ideal for soil-filled walls as the stems quickly re-grow binding the sides together with their roots. To prevent it from taking over and squeezing out the wild flowers, prune back the fresh stems that appear through the summer with shears. Also, connect a hose to the irrigation pipe in periods of drought, leaving it on for an hour at a time to ensure all the soil inside the wall gets a good soak.

6 Lay micro irrigation pipe the length of the wall, tying up one end and feeding the end with a hose pipe adaptor discreetly through the side.

7 Having covered the hose pipe with soil, doming it up above the height of the sides, lay turf along the top.

8 Finally, fill the pockets between each layer of willow rods with a mixture of wildflower seeds, such as foxgloves (Digitalis).

window in HEDGE

A circular window will instantly give hedges character, colour and charm. In gardens made sombre by shady tall hedges, a window will instantly brighten up their face and lift the shadow they cast.

1 The window frame is supported in the hedge on an H-shaped timber mount, which consists of two uprights cut at 100mm (4in) above the height you want the centre of the window and a crosspiece that is cut to the width of the window frame. Mark the position of the crosspiece by laying the uprights on level ground and setting the window between them with its centre 100mm (4in) below their tops. Fix the crosspiece below the window using L-shaped brackets and wood screws.

2 The feet of the mount are held in the hedge with fence spikes, which can be hammered into the line of the hedge without causing excessive root disturbance. Make sure that the fence spikes are spaced to the same width as the mount (if the trunks of the hedge plants correspond with the spikes, position them

MATERIALS

75mm (3in) fence spikes
75mm (3in) posts
Gable end/circular window
100mm (4in) screws
Four L-shaped brackets
Dark wood stain for posts
Glass paint or stained glass (optional)

TOOLS

Masonry and bricklaying tools
Cross cutting saw
Drill driver and pilot bit
Fence post driver

1 Make an H-shaped mount for the window using 75mm (3in) fence posts fixed together with L-shaped brackets.

2 Hammer the two fence spikes the width of the mount apart into the line of the hedge.

KNOW YOUR MATERIALS

The most economical way to buy a circular window is from a salvage yard. The condition can be variable, so check over the frame to make sure that the woodwork is sound. Don't worry if the glass is broken as this is cheaper and easier to replace than damaged spars or a rotten timber. Clean up the glass and replace any cracked sections, and then give the frame a coat of wood preserver to protect it from the weather.

3 Secure the window onto the crosspiece by pilot drilling angled holes through the window frame into the uprights.

just in front of the trees) and use a fence post driver to protect their tops as you hammer. In hedges with dense foliage, it is easier to construct the mount in situ by tapping the uprights into the fence spikes and then attaching the crosspiece in the hedge. To help disguise the timber, paint with a black or dark brown wood stain.

3 Rest the window onto the crosspiece and secure by pilot drilling angled holes through the face of the window frame into the uprights and fixing with 100mm (4in) screws.

Tie branches that block the window back with string and hide the mount by pulling foliage in front of it. Any branches that obscure the glass and are too big to tie back, prune with loppers. After installing the window, the hedge will need a few months to grow round it completely. To encourage this process, water and feed during the growing season, clipping when necessary.

entrances

planning for entrances

Opening a gate onto a garden should be meditative and romantic, exchanging the hurly-burly of outside life for peace and tranquillity. It's the catalyst for relaxation or to embark on that most pleasurable of activities, gardening. Although a gate's function is essentially about providing access, it also welcomes, frames the view of the garden beyond and engenders a sense of exploration.

Function and style Access might be the primary reason for designing an entrance in a boundary, but it is not always its most important function. You can place entrances even where they are not needed to separate different areas and thereby create a feeling of space. A cleverly placed gate can lead you on a whole new axis, imparting a sense of direction and mystery to your garden. It can also make areas seem more secluded and secret, enabling you to develop completely separate themes, even in fairly small spaces.

A door can bring a feeling of quality, especially if it's heavy and decorated with ironwork. Whether open or closed, it's a full stop between a front and back garden. Of course, in the broadest sense of the word, an entrance needn't be a physical doorway even, but simply the thinning of a path. Traditional Japanese gardens employ the tactic of creating low arches that not only slow the pace but also make the visitor stoop to enter the next room, demanding your full attention. It's a great device for children's gardens too, for example by using a low door that only they can get through, like a shortcut to Alice's Wonderland. At the opposite end of the scale, extremely large doors can make you feel positively Lilliputian, although using outsize doors originates from castles as a device to say, 'we are powerful, don't mess with us!'

Design choices As with all boundaries, first decide whether you want it to be see-through or to act as a screen, hiding the garden beyond. See-through entrances such as ironwork gates and picket, are diverting to the eye and create a picture, while still defending the garden on the other side. They must be used with care, however, as you don't want it overlooking a patio or seating area,

A gate within a door.

Heavy iron studs.

Plain picket gate.

Arrowhead/French gothic picket.

A gate such as the bar and brace (top left), is the obvious way to demarcate an entrance, but there are other techniques, too. A choice of bamboo screening (top right) can signal a change of pace or theme, while tall brick piers (above) make for a dramatic and imposing entrance, even when the access is open.

A rusty gate placed among the flowery borders of a cottage garden is suggestive of a boundary long overgrown and smothered in blooms.

where you want privacy. More enclosing are solid gates, but even these can have peepholes or windows built-in to lighten their heavy feel.

The type of gate you choose should be dictated by the adjacent boundary. Brick and stone walls suit heavy, decorated wooden or wrought-iron doors, because the quality of the materials complements its surround. They are old materials and designs that have been used since time immemorial. You can get this look even with a fence by bolstering the density of the boundary with trellis and classic roses and ivy to give the whole structure more weight.

To make an entrance as dramatic as possible, you need to embellish the surrounds. Traditional treatments include abundant planting, particularly scented flowers which bombard your senses as you slow to open the gate. Good plants include winter-flowering *Viburnum farreri* and Christmas box (*Sarcococca*) and swags of summer roses and jasmine (*Jasminum*) which can be trained into a fragrant frame for the doorway.

If you're making a gate in a timber fence, it's appropriate to make it in a similar wood and pick out details in the boundary. To prevent the gate from being camouflaged it must be distinguished in some way. For example, in a picket fence make the posts either side slightly larger and prominent with finials and give it a convex or concave top.

You can also use paint effects to highlight the entrance. The right stain can give even cheap pine the look of weathered oak. Hinges, latches, doorsprings and bolts – collectively known as door furniture – all offer opportunity for embellishment and detail. You needn't just go for the basic type, there are many different finishes and the shapes range from elaborate Fleur-de-Lys designs and beaten ironwork to stainless steel. The size of furniture you choose may be in scale with the doorway or outsize to give the illusion of salvage, a portico that may have been cut down and rescued from a moated castle. The furniture relates to how you want the gate to work. You don't want the best side stuck against the wall if it is going to spend most of its life ajar. Also give some consideration to the direction it's going to open – which side should you have the hinges on, so it opens in the most convenient direction.

The materials you use in the gate can take their influence from the surrounding landscape. This works very well in woodland gardens where branches from the trees are apparently used in the construction.

A see-through gate allows glimpses of the garden beyond and, as such, the materials used in its manufacture must link with those visible through its louvres. For example, behind a modern metal gate (above left) you would expect to find metal planters, water features or steel grid paving, linking the view to what is in the garden. What lies behind a solid gate is a secret, unless it is propped ajar (above right) as an invitation to enter.

Beech arch.

Vine-covered gate.

Bamboo fence and gate.

Flowery tunnel.

timber DOOR

An imposing wooden door, decorated with ornamental studs and hinges, is the most grand and aristocratic of garden entrances. When closed, the robust façade creates an air of impregnability, suggesting that whatever is on the other side must be worth seeing. The click of the latch and the pleasing swing as the weighty door arcs open, tempts you through to discover the secret garden beyond.

MATERIALS

Seven oak planks from cut down railway sleepers (or timber) 22mm (⅞in) thick, 240mm (9½in) wide and at least the height of the door

Thirty two 40mm (1½in) brass screws

Ninety six 40mm (1½in) decorative nails

Twelve 75mm (3in) decorative nails

Five large decorative iron hinges

Fleur-de-Lys butterfly latch

TOOLS

Carpentry tools

Plane

Sander

Hammer

Router

Circular saw

1 Cut the planks to the height you want the door and then cut them to width using a circular saw fitted with a 'fence' (a guide bar that ensures that cuts are straight). How wide the planks are depends on the width of the door, and a little maths is necessary to get this right as they aren't of equal width. When put together, all four have to be 3–4mm (⅛in) smaller than the width of the opening, but the two central planks need to be 20mm (¾in) narrower than the edge planks. This ensures that the cover strips (see step 3) that are fixed over the joints between the planks are evenly spaced. To get this right, cut a strip of timber that's the width of the opening and mark the position of each plank and cover strip to ensure that their spacing is correct. If you are using reclaimed timber, save the soundest planks for the ledges (see step 2) and check for

1 Using a circular saw, cut the planks to the required width. Remove any lumps and bumps with a plane.

2 Evenly space five ledges to the back of the door and secure them to the planks with brass screws.

KNOW YOUR MATERIALS

The oak planks used for this door were once tar-covered railway sleepers, bolted to tracks and pummelled by passing trains. Despite this ignominious past, the oak (which was used before pine became ubiquitous) looks as good as if it was cut for the purpose. The only tell-tale sign is the odd bolt-hole where the rails were once secured to the sleepers. Cut-down sleepers are available from salvage yards. For suppliers, see page 126. Always buy decorative nails and door furniture that have been coated with rustproof paint. This stops corrosion and prevents tannins in the oak reacting with the iron, which would cause grey stains to appear on the face of the door.

straightness. Use a plane where necessary to remove any lumps and bumps.

2 The ledges, which are fixed to the back of the door, hold the door together. Their length is the same width as the door and they can be any width, although to look more in scale, they should be 20–30mm (¾–1in) thinner than the planks used for the face of the door and have their edges rounded with a sander.

To create an ancient heavy look, evenly space five ledges on the back of the door leaving a slightly larger gap between the bottom of the door and the first ledge. Secure them with two brass screws in each plank (always pilot and countersink the holes first). Although the brass looks bright, it won't take long before it weathers down to the colour of oak.

3 The cover strips are made by cutting a plank down into 45mm (1¾in) strips with a circular saw. You need three to cover the joints on the face of the door and enough to make a surround for the door's edge. Clamp each strip to a work bench and using a router, cut a C-shaped bevel along both edges of the three central cover strips. Then bevel one side of the two longest edging strips leaving the top and bottom strip as they are.

4 Lay the top strip in position on the face of the door and check that it is square, then fix with evenly spaced 40mm (1½in) decorative nails (in this project four were used). Always drill a pilot hole for the nails first, otherwise the wood will split.

5 Cut the central cover strips to length (they should be the height of the door minus the width of the top and bottom strips). Support the door on timber battens and butt the cover strips against the top edge strip and fix with 75mm (3in) decorative nails driven through the gaps and through the ledges. Flip the door over and bend the centimetre (half inch) of nail that protrudes through the door with hammer.

3 *Clamp each cover strip to a work bench and use a router to cut a C-shaped bevel along both edges of the three central strips.*

4 *Put the top edge strip in position and check that is it square before fixing to the planks with evenly spaced decorative nails.*

5 *Having cut the central cover strips to length butt them against the top edge strip and fix with decorative nails.*

As the nails are hammered over, the cover strips are pulled tightly into the door. Then flip the door back over and fit the edge strips with their bevelled corner facing towards the centre of the door and finally the strip along the bottom of the door. Pilot all nail holes before hammering.

6 Make a cardboard template to locate the positions of the decorative nails between the cover strips and over the ledges. Pilot drill holes through the template before hammering home the 40mm (1½in) nails.

7 On old doors, the hinges are always set beneath the ledges. To enhance the olde worlde look use five, one screwed beneath each ledge. Another design option is to use two sizes of hinges with three 300mm (12in) hinges in the middle and two 450mm (18in) hinges at the top and bottom of the door. Doing this gives the door a brawny appearance much the same as the hinges of a treasure chest.

8 Position the door in the opening and prop it on wooden wedges while you screw the hinges to the frame. Any sides that stick can be sanded down once the door is hung. Finally, fit the butterfly latch to the door and the catch on the frame.

Alternative materials and designs

The feel and appearance of oak is hard to match but if you want to save money, you can get pretty close to it with pine. If you use pine, once the door has been built give it a coat of oak-effect wood stain to darken it down and to protect it from the weather.

No matter what timber you use, if it is to look in keeping, an 'antique' door must be set into an appropriate opening, like the brick piers used here. If you have only fences, it would work if you disguised the edges with ivy or heavy trellis. Alternatively, cut an opening in a hedge.

When hammering nails home, support the underside of the door with a brick to soak up the vibration.

6 Make a cardboard template to position decorative nails between the cover strips and over the ledges.

7 Set large decorative iron hinges, coated in rustproof paint to prevent corrosion, beneath each ledge.

8 Position the door in the opening and prop it up on wooden wedges while you screw the hinges to the frame.

rustic GATE

Touching the bark of trees never fails to send a tingle to my fingers and that's part of the appeal of this birch gate. The natural materials and homespun, yeoman style perfectly capture the spirit of the garden with its silver birch and the clouds of cow parsley that surround it. Where an off-the-peg gate could easily jar in such a natural setting, its pale pickets look as if they have swung in the dappled shade for years.

MATERIALS

5m (16ft) of 50 x 50mm (2 x 2in) rough sawn tanalized timber

50mm (2in) screws

Birch poles or similar branches in diameters of 20–50mm (¾–2in)

L-shaped metal brackets (optional)

Hinges and latch

TOOLS

Wood saw

Drill and pilot bit

Chisel and mallet

Garden loppers

1 Gates are susceptible to wear and tear, and because of this it is important to have a sturdy frame. To make the frame, cut two lengths 50 x 50mm (2 x 2in) timber to the width of the opening less 5mm (¼in) to allow the gate to open. Cut another two lengths to make the uprights (in this project they were 750mm/30in) and cut half-lap joints in the ends of the timber by sawing and chiselling halfway through the timbers where they meet (for details see page 26) and screw together. As an alternative to half-lap joints you can use L-shaped metal brackets to hold the corners together.

2 Make the X-shaped brace for the centre of the gate by laying two lengths of 50 x 50mm (2 x 2in) timber diagonally across the frame and marking where they meet the inside edge. Cut at this point and check that each length fits snugly into the frame. Join them

1 Having worked out the measurements of the frame, cut the timber to the required lengths and screw the pieces together.

2 Next make the X-shaped brace for the centre of the gate. Cut two lengths of timber and mark where they meet the inside edge.

KNOW YOUR MATERIALS

Of course, birch isn't the only timber suitable for a rustic garden gate; any wood that looks appropriate in the setting will work. Hazel, beech, sycamore and even conifer branches (with leaves removed) are all in keeping, more so if they are prunings from trees that grow in your own garden. If you want to create the effect of white birch bark, there are wood stains available in silver birch colours, which protect the timber too. Birch is a very soft wood, but you can overcome its susceptibility to rot by keeping it out of contact with the soil and giving it the occasional coat of linseed oil or wood preservative.

3 Work out the spacing of the birch lengths and screw them in place. Use a saw or garden loppers to cut off the top.

together by marking where they cross and saw halfway through the timber at this point. Remove the timber between the cuts with a chisel. As an easier alternative, it is perfectly acceptable although less attractive to use just one brace. Ensure that it runs diagonally up from the hinge side of the gate to give maximum support to the frame.

3 Lay the lengths of birch onto the frame and when you're happy with their spacing, pilot and screw in place. It's a good idea to prop the gate in position as a visual aid when you are deciding the most appropriate height for the tops before marking and cutting the birch to length. In this project the tops were cut with a domed top that arched above the frame by 75–150mm (3–6in) to highlight the position of the gate, but a concave or staggered top would look just as good. You can use a saw or garden loppers to do this. Fit hinges and a latch to the frame and hang in position.

index

suppliers

The publisher and photographer would like to thank the following for permission to take photographs of their gardens.

(NGS: indicates a garden is open under the National Garden Scheme)

Broadlands Garden, Dorset p8

The Burystead Courtyard Garden, Sutton, Cambs p78–79

Cambridge University Botanic Garden p100–101, 102 bottom left, 103 top right, 105 bottom 3rd from left

Capel Manor Gardens, Enfield p10 bottom left

John Drake, Fen Ditton, Cambs p102 bottom 3rd from left, 104 top

Bob & Sue Foulser, Cerne Abbas, Dorset p115 bottom

Marlas Greiger, Howell, Michigan, USA p116

Hookwood Farmhouse, West Horsley, Surrey p9 top right, 112–113, 116 bottom left

Robinson College, Cambridge p6–7, 11 top centre, 102 bottom right, 103 bottom

Trinity College, Cambridge p105 top right, 105 bottom right

The Walnuts, King's Cliffe, Northants p11 bottom right, 39 top left, 39 top right

The author would like to thank the following for their assistance in supplying materials.

Rowlinson Garden Products Ltd, Weston Road, Crewe, Cheshire CW1 6FZ; tel: 01270 506 903 www.rowgar.co.uk Suppliers of new railway sleepers, deck, wattle hurdle and smart panel fencing.

Ridgeons Builders Merchants; tel: 01223 466 000 Suppliers of bricks, timber, concrete blocks, fencing materials inluding feather boards and split chestnut pales.

Mackays Metals Warehouse All metals including sheet copper. 85 East Road, Cambridge CB1 1BY tel: 01223 517 000

Solopark plc Station Road, nr Pampisford; tel: 01223 834 663 www.solopark.co.uk Suppliers of reclaimed and new building materials including sawn railway sleepers, reclaimed bricks and reclaimed windows.

Tropical Surrounds The Old Grain Store, Redenham Park Farm, Redenham, nr Andover, Hampshire SP11 9AQ; tel: 01264 773 006 Suppliers of bamboo and other exciting screens and claddings.

Travis Perkins Tool Hire; tel: 0870 607 8700 www.toolmart.co.uk For big and small, time-saving hire equipment.

Clayton Monroe Ltd, Kingston West Drive, Kingston, Staverton, Totnes, Devon TQ9 6AR http://www.claytonmunroe.com Hinges, latches, hooks and you name it!

Out of the Woods, 8 Kimbolton Road, Bedford MK40 2NR; tel: 01234 269 641; outofthewoods@cooperj54.fsnet.co.uk Suppliers of willow wands, hazel rods and birch poles.

Bannold Supplies, Bannold Road, Waterbeach, Cambridge; tel: 0500 012 231 For dressed York stone and slate (plus numerous other stones).

Tinsley Wire Ltd, PO Box 119, Shepcote Lane, Sheffield S9 1TY; Suppliers of gabions. tel: 0114 2561 561 www.weldmesh.co.uk

Scotsdales Garden Centre, 120 Cambridge Road, Great Shelford, Cambridge; tel: 01223 842 777 For top-quality greenery.

Metpost, Mardy Road, Cardiff, South Glamorgan CF3 8EX; tel: 02920 777 877 www.metpost.co.uk For sockets, spike driving tools, spikes, feet and post extenders in all sizes.

author's acknowledgements

I'd like to thank Anna Osborn, Iain MacGregor and all the Murdoch team for their hard work. John Cooper from Out of the Woods and my brother Barry for being such troopers; Laurie and Susan Hartman and Peter and Amanda Dalby for the use of their gardens. Howard Rice for the laughs and his fab photography and my beautiful wife Lisa for her genius.

First published in 2001 by Murdoch Books UK Ltd

ISBN 1 85391 868 7

A catalogue record for this book is available from the British Library.

Commissioning Editor: **Iain MacGregor**

Editors: **Selina Mumford and Dawn Henderson**

Designer: **Cathy Layzell and Kenny Grant**

Managing Editor: **Anna Osborn**

Design Manager: **Helen Taylor**

Photo Librarian: **Bobbie Leah**

Photographer: **Howard Rice**

Illustrator: **Nicola Gregory**

CEO: **Robert Oerton**

Publisher: **Catie Ziller**

Production Manager: **Lucy Byrne**

International Sales Director: **Kevin Lagden**

Colour separation by Colourscan, Singapore

Printed in Singapore by Tien Wah Press

Murdoch Books UK Ltd
Ferry House, 51–57 Lacy Road,
Putney, London, SW15 1PR
Tel: +44 (0)20 8355 1480
Fax: +44 (0)20 8355 1499
Murdoch Books UK Ltd is a subsidiary
of Murdoch Magazines Pty Ltd.

UK Distribution
Macmillan Distribution Ltd
Houndsmills, Brunell Road,
Basingstoke, Hampshire, RG1 6XS
Tel: +44 (0)1256 302 707
Fax: +44 (0)1256 351 437
http://www.macmillan-mdl.co.uk.

Murdoch Books®
GPO Box 1203, Sydney,
NSW 1045, Australia
Tel: +61 (0)2 4352 7025
Fax: +61 (0)2 4352 7026
Murdoch Books® is a trademark
of Murdoch Magazines Pty Ltd.